The Garden of the Prophet
Khalil Gibran

English & Arabic

Jamil Elabed

ISBN: 978-0-9928995-5-4 (Paperback)
       978-0-9928995-6-1 (Hardback)
       978-0-9928995-7-8 (ePub)
A catalogue record of the print edition is available from the British Library.

Cover image: Courtesy of *Tursunbaev Ruslan.*
Cover design: Courtesy of *Samantha Pearce.*

Jamil Elabed is a Syrian-British translator. In 1994, he worked as a broadcast
journalist in the Arabic branch of the BBC World Service. In 1998, he published the
first edition of his translation of Gibran's The Prophet. He won the EU Creative
Translation Award followed by the British University of East Anglia's Translation
Residency Grant. He has been a full member of the Institute of Translation and
Interpreting (ITI) since 2000. Jamil taught Translation and Interpreting at Leeds
University while freelancing as a professional conference interpreter.

Preface

We see so little of Nature beyond the exterior, yet we never tire of employing our imagination to attempt to pierce through it; to probe the fathomless emptiness and discern the unseen.

Poetry, music, art and other spiritual and intellectual endeavours, such as contemplation and visualisation, are but some of man's abstract vessels for roaming the distances between the earth and the heavens in search of the beginnings. Through these cosmic lenses, we hope to reveal a glimpse of that which encompasses the great silence that may appear utterly vague and inaccessibly remote, yet at the same time feels oh so very close.

Seeking the truth is a calling. It is not some kind of psychological or spiritual craving, but an existential need that flows like the blood in human veins, hence man's innate sense of curiosity.

The secret, or the truth, is in the beginnings; in the infinite emptiness from where everything came. The severing of the attachment between man and Nature from the moment man is born remains a gaping hole in his subconscious. All the peace and melodious harmony he had been enjoying in the womb – the shell that enclosed his burgeoning understanding – are lost the moment that the umbilical cord is cut, and what follows is an unconscious craving for the beginning, for the very first bond with Nature, which was all peace and harmony; an unbreakable existential bond. That craving takes the form of sparking curiosity, man's undying lust for knowledge; the first knowledge, back when knowledge was soul, for the mind is but a tool, just like imagination is a tool that Nature designed for man to navigate through the First Day of life, to serve man in his or her existential detachment.

However, that very first knowledge is fingerprinted on the walls of man's heart. It never ceases to inspire him. It is the far and the near, the out and the in; the quantum that is everything. For Nature, which created man, never abandons him. She is the realm of all realms. She knows no boundaries. She is Mother.

Reunion with Nature is man's greatest insurmountable urge, which manifests itself through dreams and art more than in anything else. All there is tells us of all there is, albeit vaguely, while we passionately yearn for our timeless attachment.

Every womb came from a greater womb. Even the infinite emptiness from which all came is but a womb. Man's sense of things has roots. Those roots were the beginning. The womb that furnished man with sense and intellect was the first womb. The womb that gave man the body is only the Sperm Womb, the second womb; the life-developed womb where man's ethereal quantum is now safely housed.

Man's detachment at birth is akin to his exodus from the infinite emptiness of heaven. It set him on route to explore the wonders and miracles of being, and to baptise him into the House of God, the womb of all wombs; the sepulchre of holiness; the ultimate rising.

The infinite emptiness surrounds us like the midday sun. While we feel and think of the vast distance now separating us from the truth, we are still surrounded by her; she is in the silent knowledge of our heart. Exploring the truth in man's fathomless depths is an exercise in ecstasy and joy, for it is the ultimate journey towards the Big Reunion.

The Prophet and *The Garden of the Prophet* are two stations on the same voyage; the inevitable pilgrimage to the holy mountain, like the cloud in dark skies journeying to the light of day.

Man came from the mist and is apt to return to the mist. That is what *The Garden of the Prophet* is about.

Jamil Elabed

Gibran's English Text Finds Its Legitimate Arabic Counterpart at Last

By Professor Boutros Al-Hallaq
Teacher of Contemporary Arabic Literature,
Sorbonne University, Paris, France

While reading Jamil Elabed's translation, I was struck by the realisation that there is a missing link between Gibran's two sides: Gibran the writer in Arabic and Gibran the writer in English. This came following a long-lasting schizophrenia that made the author of *The Prophet* a sovereign persona within Gibran's mind, through which alone his genius was manifest, as a result of the injustice done to the first side and the curtailment and distortion of the second.

Jamil has not translated so much as discovered what went on in Gibran's thoughts, as the latter constructed his work in a language not his own. He has striven to give voice to Gibran's freewheeling heartbeats in his mother tongue, and he has done so with palpable spontaneity in an English text that, like the act of translating itself, is expected to fall short of capturing the full extent of the intrinsic ingenuity that the man from Mount Lebanon possessed.

It is clear that Jamil has called upon his extensive experience and then poured it into Gibran's mother tongue, which he himself fully masters in all its aspects and details. I dare say he crafted it; that is to say, he fashioned it in such a way that the full range of meaning has been conveyed in exactly the way that Gibran envisioned at the time (yes, at that very time). However, Jamil has not frozen Gibran's Arabic-language writing style in its original dated mould, but has rather refashioned it into an enhanced, yet still utterly Gibranic, modern form. This version has been enriched by so many years of creative input and contemplation, but still it remains faithful to Gibran's matchless singular vision. The distinct style of Gibran in his forties is very much in evidence here, and yet there are also obvious differences, as though the text has ripened with age. The themes that permeate his Arabic compositions are all present, with Jamil's choice of words perfectly reflecting those of Gibran wherever author and translator intersect.

I do admit that I found in Jamil's text, without him knowing, strong support for my consistent belief that from the first word he wrote in Arabic to the last word he wrote in English, Gibran's world never changes. His was a perspective that emanated from a unique, exceptional and extraordinary sense that he derived from the geography of the Levant which he belonged to. It also springs from his inherited and time-honoured Arabic culture, which he drank from and traced down deep, perceiving it in an outstandingly dynamic manner.

The formation of Gibran's world sprung from the womb of the Semitic and oriental cultures that the Levant witnessed over thousands of years, and this momentum gave rise to some of the greatest human narratives, namely religious and epic texts, that remained effective in the unforetold cache of the language, and the memory and fancy of the masses. If his Arabic texts were always sourced from this rich reservoir of culture, it goes without saying that his English texts were also born from the womb of his Arabic inspiration, albeit in a different cultural context and a specific human era.

Our true Arabic culture is unlike anything perceived by literary scholars and linguists of old, or even present-day intellectuals, and I have no doubt that Gibran was a trailblazer when it came to unearthing the treasured essence of our exquisite, world-class Arab culture. Most certainly, he was more than just a social reformer, and also far removed from the concept of popular prophetism that is beyond humanism. He was but a human being in flesh and blood, just like us. He probed the meaning of how to *be* part and parcel of all times, yet avoided the trap of nationalistic and dogmatic chauvinism, and the concept of progress based on mere intellectualism, which almost always leads to sheer enslavement.

Gibran is the human reagent for the dynamic outpouring of our cultural resources, which are as vast as the Levant's history and geography. He is also possibly the one who most accurately mirrors our farthest dreams, not just as Levant-Arabs, but also as partners in the collective imagination of modern people, whatever their culture, religion and ideology; those who long to end the rift and cross the distance between the mind and the heart, between reason and passion, and between technical advancement and human elevation.

Don't we agree with Gibran that beingness is a progressive movement that never stops, and that life is an everlasting genesis towards completeness?

Now, about the translation, I say to him, *what a beautiful translation this is, Jamil!*

Boutros Hallaq
Paris, 21 November 2019

For Greta Thunberg

Contents

The Garden of the Prophet

AL MUSTAFA, THE CHOSEN AND THE beloved who was a noon upon his own day, returned to the isle of his birth in the month of Tichreen, which is the month of remembrance.

And as his ship approached the harbour, he stood upon its prow, and his mariners were about him. And there was a homecoming in his heart.

And he spoke, and the sea was in his voice, and he said:

"Behold, the isle of our birth. Even here the earth heaved us, a song and a riddle; a song unto the sky, a riddle unto the earth; and what is there between earth and sky that shall carry the song and solve the riddle save our own passion?

آبٌ المصطفى، المختار الحبيب وضحى نهاره، إلى ربوع ميلاده في تشرين، شهر التذكر والحنين.

وإذ دنت سفينته من المرفأ وقف على مقدمها، وبحارته حوله، تهزج في قلبه نواقيس العودة.

وتكلم، والبحر بعض من نبرته، وقال:

"انظروا، هنا ولدت. هنا جاشت الأرض بي، أغنية ولغزاً؛ أغنية للسماء، لغزاً للأرض؛ وماذا بين الأرض والسماء ما سيحمل الأغنية ويحل اللغز إلا ما يملأ جوارحي من وجد؟

"The sea yields us once more to these shores. We are but another wave of her waves. She sends us forth to sound her speech, but how shall we do so unless we break the symmetry of our heart on rock and sand?

"For this is the law of mariners and the sea. If you would freedom, you must needs turn to mist. The formless is forever seeking form, even as the countless nebulae would become suns and moons; and we who have sought much and return now to the isle, rigid moulds, we must become mist once more and learn of the beginning. And what is there that shall live and rise unto the heights except it be broken unto passion and freedom?

"إلى هذه الشطآن ثانية يقذفني البحر. ما أنا إلا موجة أخرى من موجاته. يرسلني لأردد كلامه، وكيف لي إن لم أكسر نسَق قلبي على صخر ورمل؟"

"ذلك هو قانون البحارة والبحر. إن كنت تصبو إلى الحرية، فصِر إلى ضباب. عديم الشكل إلى الأبد يبحث عن شكل، كما السُدم التي لا تعد، تصير إلى شموس وأقمار؛ وأنا الذي بحثت طويلاً وأعود الآن يابس الأطراف إلى المهد، علي أن أصير ضباباً وأتعلم من البَدء. وهل من يحيا ويرقى إلى الذرى إن لم ينكسر ويثُب إلى حرية ووجد؟

"For ever shall we be in quest of the shores that we may sing and be heard. But what of the wave that breaks where no ear shall hear? It is the unheard in us that nurses our deeper sorrow. Yet it is also the unheard which carves our soul to form and fashion our destiny."

Then one of his mariners came forth and said:

"Master, you have captained our longing for this harbour, and behold, we have come. Yet you speak of sorrow, and of hearts that shall be broken."

And he answered him and said:

"Did I not speak of freedom, and of the mist which is your greater freedom? Yet it is in pain I make pilgrimage to the isle where I was born, even like unto a ghost of one slain come to kneel before those who have slain him."

"أبداً سأبحث عن الشطآن لأغني ولتصل أغنياتي السمع. لكن ماذا عن الموجة تتكسر ولا تسمعها أذن؟ ما لا يُسمَع في داخلي أداري به أعمق الحزن. وهذا الذي لا يسمع أيضاً يجترح مع ذلك روحي لتشكل وتصوغ قدري."

ثم تقدم أحد بحارته وقال له:

"سيدي، قدتَ شراع شوقنا إلى هذا المرفأ، وانظر، لقد وصلنا. لكنك تتكلم عن الحزن، وعن قلوب ستتكسر."

فأجابه وقال:

"ألم أتحدث عن الحرية، وعن الضباب الذي هو حريتك الأعظم؟ لكني أحج إلى حيث ولدت، يعتريني ألم، كروح ذبيحٍ جاء يجثو أمام قاتله."

And another mariner spoke and said:

"Behold the multitudes on the sea-wall. In their silence they have foretold even the day and the hour of your coming, and they have gathered from their fields and vineyards in their loving need, to await you."

And Almustafa looked afar upon the multitudes, and his heart was mindful of their yearning, and he was silent.

Then a cry came from the people, and it was a cry of remembrance and entreaty.

وتكلم بحار آخر وقال:

"انظرِ الجموع على سور البحر. في صمتهم تنبأوا حتى بيوم وساعة وصولك، ولقد تجمعوا من حقولهم وكرومهم يحدوهم شوق المحب، لانتظارك."

مد المصطفى بصره بعيداً إلى الحشود، وقلبُه عالِمٌ بشوقهم، وران عليه صمت.

وإذ بصيحة يطلقها الخلق، صيحة استذكار وتضرع.

And he looked upon his mariners and said:

"And what have I brought them? A hunter was I, in a distant land. With aim and might I have spent the golden arrows they gave me, but I have brought down no game. I followed not the arrows. Mayhap they are spreading now in the sun with the pinions of wounded eagles that would not fall to earth. And mayhap the arrow heads have fallen into the hands of those who had need of them for bread and wine.

'I know not where they have spent their flight, but this I know: they have made their curve in the sky.

نظر إلى بحارته وقال:

"بماذا أنا عائد إليهم؟ صياداً كنت، في بلاد بعيدة. أطلقت السهام الذهبية التي أعطَونيها، بسداد وقوة، لكني ما اصطدت طريدة. لم أتعقب السهام. ربما تراها الآن متناثرة في الشمس مع أجنحة نسور جريحة أبت السقوط إلى الأرض. ولربما سقطت رؤوسها بأيد تحتاجها لنبيذ وخبز.

"لا أعرف إلى أي منتهى حلقت، لكنني أعرف أنها نفّذت منعرجها في السماء.

"Even so, love's hand is still upon me, and you, my mariners, still sail my vision, and I shall not be dumb. I shall cry out when the hand of the seasons is upon my throat, and I shall sing my words when my lips are burned with flames."

And they were troubled in their hearts because he spoke these things. And one said:

"Master, teach us all, and mayhap because your blood flows in our veins, and our breath is of your fragrance, we shall understand."

"رغم هذا، يد الحب مازالت على كتفي، وأنتم، بحارتي، مازلتم تبحرون برؤاي، ولن أكون أخرسَ. سأرفع صوتي ما أن تلمس يد الفصول حنجرتي، وسأغني كلماتي ما أن تتوهج باللهيب شفتاي."

اضطربت القلوب لسماع هذا الكلام. أحدهم قال:

"سيدي، علمنا، دمك يجري في عروقنا، وأنفاسنا بعض من شذاك، فلربما نفهم."

Then he answered them, and the wind was in his voice, and he said:

"Brought you me to the isle of my birth to be a teacher? Not yet have I been caged by wisdom. Too young am I and too verdant to speak of aught but self, which is forever the deep calling upon the deep.

"Let him who would have wisdom seek it in the buttercup or in a pinch of red clay. I am still the singer.

"Still I shall sing the earth, and I shall sing your lost dreaming that walks the day between sleep and sleep. But I shall gaze upon the sea."

فأجابهم، والريح في صوته، وقال:

"أجئتم بي إلى مرابع مولدي كي أكون معلماً؟ لم تُحِط الحكمة بي بعد. مازلت غضاً لأتحدث في أي أمر، اللهم إلا النفس، العمق الذي ينادي العمق.

"دعوا طالب الحكمة يبحث عنها في الحَوذان الأصفر أو في درَّة صلصال. أنا المغني لأزال.

"سأظل أغني الأرض، وأحلامَكم الضائعةَ تجوب النهار بين نوم ونوم. لكن سأرنو إلى البحر."

And now the ship entered the harbour and reached the sea-wall, and he came thus to the isle of his birth and stood once more amongst his own people. And a great cry arose from their hearts so that the loneliness of his homecoming was shaken within him.

And they were silent awaiting his word, but he answered them not, for the sadness of memory was upon him, and he said in his heart:

"Have I said that I shall sing? Nay, I can but open my lips that the voice of life may come forth and go out to the wind for joy and support."

ولجت السفينة الميناءَ وحاذت سور البحر، وإذا به على الأرض التي أنجبته يقف ثانية بين أهله. وصعدت من القلوب صيحة عظيمة أرعشت فيه إحساس الوِحدة الذي لازمه أثناء عودته.

وصمت الناس بانتظار كلمته، لكنه لم يجب صمتهم، فحزن الذكرى يغمره، وقال في سره:

"هل قلت إني سأغني؟ أجل، ما علي إلا أن أفلق شفتي فيفترّ منهما صوت الحياة قاصداً الريحَ لفرح ومَدد."

Then Karima, she who had played with him, a child, in the Garden of his mother, spoke and said:

"Twelve years have you hidden your face from us, and for twelve years have we hungered and thirsted for your voice."

And he looked upon her with exceeding tenderness, for it was she who had closed the eyes of his mother when the white wings of death had gathered her.

And he answered and said:

"Twelve years? Said you twelve years, Karima? I measured not my longing with the starry rod, nor did I sound the depth thereof. For love when love is homesick exhausts time's measurements and time's soundings.

ثم تكلمت كريمة التي لعبت معه في حديقة أمه طفلاً،
وقالت:

"اثني عشر عاماً حرمتَنا من رؤية محياك، ولاثني عشر
عاماً تضورت قلوبنا لسماع صوتك تضورَ جائع ظمآن."

ببالغ الحنان رنا إليها، فهي من أطبق عيني أمه حين
ضمتها أجنحة الموت البيضاء.

وأجاب وقال:

"اثنا عشرعاماً؟ هل قلتِ اثني عشر عاماً، يا كريمة؟ لم
أقِس أنا شوقي بعصاً، ولم أسبِر عمقَه بمِرنان. فالحب إذا
عصف الشوق به، لا تكفي لقياسه مقاييس الزمان.

"There are moments that hold aeons of separation. Yet parting is naught but an exhaustion of the mind. Perhaps we have not parted."

And Almustafa looked upon the people, and he saw them all, the youth and the aged, the stalwart and the puny, those who were ruddy with the touch of wind and sun, and those who were of pallid countenance; and upon their face a light of longing and of questioning.

And one spoke and said:

"Master, life has dealt bitterly with our hopes and our desires. Our hearts are troubled, and we do not understand. I pray you, comfort us, and open to us the meanings of our sorrow."

"هناك لحظات تضوي دهورَ فراق. والفراق كلٌ يصيب العقل. ربما لم تفرقنا الأيام."

ونظر المصطفى إلى الناس، المسن والشاب، الزهيد والمقدام، ومن تورد خده بلفح الشمس ولثمِ الريح، ومن بهِت لونُه وشحُب مرآه؛ وعلى الوجوه رمَح نور شوق وبريق سؤال.

وتكلم أحدهم وقال:

"أيها المعلم، أذاقت الحياة آمالنا وأشواقنا مُرَّ الهوان. قلوبنا اضطربت، وبات الفهم بعيد المنال. أستحلفك، أرحنا، وفك لنا معاني الأحزان."

And his heart was moved with compassion, and he said:

'Life is older than all things living; even as beauty was winged ere the beautiful was born on earth, and even as truth was truth ere it was uttered.

"Life sings in our silences, and dreams in our slumber. Even when we are beaten and low, Life is enthroned and high. And when we weep, Life smiles upon the day; and is free even when we drag our chains.

"Oftentimes we call Life bitter names, but only when we ourselves are bitter and dark. And we deem her empty and unprofitable, but only when the soul goes wandering in desolate places, and the heart is drunken with over-mindfulness of self.

تحرك لاعج قلبه، فقال:

"قبل كل حي كانت الحياة؛ ولقد كان للجمال جناح قبل أن يولد الجميل على الأرض، حتى الحقيقة كانت الحقيقة قبل أن ينطِق بها لسان.

"في سكنات صمتنا تغني الحياة، وتحلم إذ ننام. وإذ نُغلَبُ ونَغتَم، تضع تاجها وتسمو الحياة. وإذ نبكي، تبتسم للنهار؛ وحرة تبقى حتى حينما تجرجر أقدامنا الأغلال.

"نطلق على الحياة لاذع الأسماء في الأحيان، ذلك حين تكتنفنا ظلمةٌ ويجتاحنا مرار. ولا نخالها فارغة وناضبة إلا عندما تهيم الروح في القفار، ويسكر القلب مختالاً بالذات.

23

"Life is deep and high and distant, and though only your vast vision can reach even her feet, yet she is near; and though only the breath of your breath reaches her heart, the shadow of your shadow crosses her face, and the echo of your faintest cry becomes a spring and an autumn in her breast.

"And Life is veiled and hidden, even as your greater self is hidden and veiled. Yet when Life speaks, all the winds become words; and when she speaks again, the smiles upon your lips and the tears in your eyes turn also into words. When she sings, the deaf hear and are held; and when she comes walking, the sightless behold her and are amazed and follow her in wonder and astonishment."

"عميقة وسَنِيّة وقَصِيَّة هي الحياة، ورغم أن قدمها لا يصله إلا أبعد رؤاك، فهي قريبة منك؛ ورغم أن قلبها لا يبلغه من أنفاسك إلا فَوحُ الأنفاس، فإن وجهها يعبره ظِلُ ظِلِك، وفي صدرها– من نداءاتك، يغدو ربيعاً ويغدو خريفاً صدى أوهنِ نداء.

"مِثلُ ذاتك الأكبر، خفية ومحتجبة هي الحياة. فإن تكلمت، كل الرياح تغدو كلمات؛ وإن تكلمت ثانية، كل الابتسامات على شفتيك وكل الدموع في عينيك تتحول إلى كلمات. عندما تغني يسمع الأصم ويصغي للغناء؛ وعندما تخطر، يبصرها الأعمى ذاهلاً ويمشي وراءها بعجب واندهاش."

And he ceased from speaking, and a vast silence enfolded the people, and in the silence there was an unheard song, and they were comforted of their loneliness and their aching.

And he left them straightway and followed the path which led to his Garden, which was the Garden of his mother and his father, wherein they lay asleep, they and their forefathers.

And there were those who would have followed after him, seeing that it was a home-coming, and he was alone, for there was no one left of all his kin to spread the feast of welcome, after the manner of his people.

وتوقف عن الكلام، وعم الصمت المكان، وفي الصمت انداحت أغنية لا تسمعها الآذان، أزالت الوحشة وأذهبتِ الأحزان.

وسرعان ما غادر ميمماً شطر الطريق المؤدية إلى حديقته، التي كانت حديقة أمه وأبيه، وفيها مع أجدادهما يرقدان.

وكان ثمة من أراد اللحاق به، إذ رأوا غائباً يعود ورأوه وحيداً لم يبق مِن أقاربه مَن يقيم له وليمة استقبال، جرياً على عادة البلاد.

But the captain of his ship counselled them saying:

"Suffer him to go upon his way. For his bread is the bread of aloneness, and in his cup is the wine of remembrance, which he would drink alone."

And his mariners held their steps, for they knew it was even as the captain of the ship had told them. And all those who gathered upon the sea-wall restrained the feet of their desire.

Only Karima went after him, a little way, yearning over his aloneness and his memories. And she spoke not, but turned and went unto her own house, and in the garden under the almond-tree she wept, yet she knew not wherefore.

غير أن ربان سفينته أشار عليهم بقوله:

"دعوه بدربه. خبزُه خبزُ وِحدة، وخمرة الذكرى تملأ كأسه،
ويريد أن يرشفها لوحده."

أطفأ البحارة أوار اندفاعهم نحوه، إذ أدركوا صواب ما قاله
الربان. وكبح المحتشدون على سور البحر مراجل شوقهم له.

وحدها كريمة مشت خلفه في تحسر على وحدته وذكرياته،
مشت خطوات. لم تتنبس، لكنها قفلت عائدة إلى بيتها، وفي
حديقتها تحت شجرة اللوز بكت، وهي لا تعرف سبب بكائها.

And Almustafa came and found the Garden of his mother and his father, and he entered in, and closed the gate that no man might come after him.

And for forty days and forty nights he dwelt alone in that house and that Garden, and none came, even unto the gate, for it was closed, and all the people knew that he would be alone.

And when the forty days and nights were ended, Almustafa opened the gate that they might come in.

And there came nine men to be with him in the Garden; three mariners from his own ship; three who had served in the Temple and three who had been his comrades in play when they were but children together. And these were his disciples.

وصل المصطفى إلى حديقة أمه وأبيه فدخلها وأغلق بابها فلا يأتي في إثره أحد.

وفي البيت والحديقة مكث أربعين يوماً وليلة لوحده لم يأته خلالها إنسان، حتى إلى البوابة، وهذه كانت مغلقة، والناس تعلم بأنه يريد أن يكون لوحده.

وفي نهاية الأربعين يوماً وليلة، فتح المصطفى البوابة لهم.

فجاء تسعة رجال ليمكثوا معه؛ ثلاثة من بحارة سفينته؛ وثلاثة من سدنة المعبد وثلاثة من رفاق لعبه في طفولته. هؤلاء كانوا شيعته.

And on a morning his disciples sat around him and there were distances and remembrances in his eyes. And that disciple who was called Hafiz said unto him:

"Master, tell us of the city of Orphalese, and of that land wherein you tarried those twelve years."

And Almustafa was silent, and he looked away towards the hills and toward the vast ether, and there was a battle in his silence.

Then he said:

"My friends and road–fellows, pity the nation that is full of beliefs and empty of religion.

"Pity the nation that wears a cloth it does not weave, eats a bread it does not harvest, and drinks a wine that flows not from its own winepress.

ذات صباح تحلق شيعته حوله وفي عينيه تلوح مسافات وذكريات. أحدهم ويدعى خليلاً قال له:

"أيها المعلم، حدثنا عن مدينة أورفليس، وعن البلاد التي لبثت فيها اثني عشر عاماً."

صمت المصطفى، ومد بصره إلى التلال والأثير، وفي صمته نازعته نفسه.

ثم قال:

"يا أصدقائي ورفقة دربي، أشفقوا على الأمة التي تحفل بالمعتقدات وتخلو من الدين.

"أشفقوا على الأمة التي ترتدي ثوباً لا تنسجه، وتأكل خبزاً لا تحصده، وتشرب نبيذاً لا تعصر عنبه.

"Pity the nation that acclaims the bully as a hero, and that deems the glittering conqueror bountiful.

"Pity the nation that despises a passion in its dream, yet submits in its awakening.

"Pity the nation that raises not its voice save when it walks in a funeral, boasts not except among its ruins, and will rebel not save when its neck is laid between the sword and the block.

"Pity the nation whose statesman is a fox, whose philosopher is a juggler, and whose art is the art of patching and mimicking.

"Pity the nation that welcomes its new ruler with trumpetings, and farewells him with hootings, only to welcome another with trumpetings again.

"أشفقوا على الأمة التي تصفق للمتمرد كبطل، وتحسَب الغازيَ الدرّيَ محسناً.

"أشفقوا على الأمة التي تزدري هوى في حلمها، وفي صحوها تذعن له.

"أشفقوا على الأمة التي لا ترفع صوتها إلا في جنازة، ولا تتباهى إلا بين أطلالها، ولا تهُبّ إلا عندما يوضَع عنقها تحت المقصلة.

"أشفقوا على الأمة التي زعيمها ثعلب وفيلسوفها أفاك، وفنُّها فنُ رَتقٍ ومحاكاة.

"أشفقوا على الأمة التي تستقبل حاكمها بالتزمير، وتودعه بالصفير، لتستقبل غيره بالزمر من جديد.

"Pity the nation whose sages are dumb with years and whose strong men are yet in the cradle.

"Pity the nation divided into fragments, each fragment deeming itself a nation.'

And one said:

"Speak to us of that which is moving in your own heart even now."

And he looked upon that one, and there was in his voice a sound like a star singing and he said:

"In your waking dream, when you are hushed and listening to your deeper self, your thoughts, like snow-flakes, fall and flutter and garment all the sounds of your spaces with white silence.

"أشفقوا على الأمة التي أبكمت حكماءَها السنون وأقوياؤها في المهد لايزالون.

"أشفقوا على الأمة تفتت أجزاءً، كل جزء يرى نفسه أمة."

وقال أحدهم:

"حدثنا عما يمور في قلبك الساعة."

نظر إلى الرجل، وقال بصوت كغناء نجم:

"في حلمك يتمطى في صحوه، حين يلجمك الصمت وأنت تصغي لعميق ذاتك، تتسّاقط أفكارُك، كنُدَف الثلج، مرفرفةً، وبصمت أبيضَ تكسو همسَ فضاءاتك.

"And what are waking dreams but clouds that bud and blossom on the sky-tree of your heart? And what are your thoughts but the petals which the winds of your heart scatter upon the hills and its fields?

"And even as you wait for peace until the formless within you takes form, so that the cloud gather and drift until the Blessed Fingers shape its grey desires to little crystal suns and moons and stars."

Then Sarkis, he who was the half-doubter spoke and said:

"But spring shall come and all the snows of our dreams and our thoughts shall melt and be no more."

"وماذا عسى الأحلامَ في صحوها أن تكون غير سحابات تتبرعم وتتفتح على عالي أغصان قلبك؟ وماذا عسى أفكارَك أن تكون إلا الأوراق التي تنثرها على التلال وحقوله رياح قلبك؟

"مَثَلُ ذلك كمَثَلِ انتظاركم السلام حتى عديم الشكل فيكم يأخذ شكلاً، فتتجمع السحابة وترحل حتى تصوغ الأصابعُ المباركة أشواقها الرمادية شموساً وأقماراً ونجوماً صغيرة صافية."

ثم تكلم مَخّول، الرجل الذي يبرح شكُّه يقينَه وقال:

"لكن نُوَّارَ سيأتي، وتذوب ثلوج أحلامنا وأفكارنا وتصبح أثراً بعد عين."

And he answered saying:

"When Spring comes to seek His beloved among the slumbering groves and vineyards, the snows shall indeed melt and shall run in streams to seek the river in the valley, to be the cup-bearer to the myrtle-trees and laurel.

"All things shall melt and turn into songs when spring comes. Even the stars, the vast snow-flakes that fall slowly upon the larger fields, shall melt into singing streams. When the sun of His face shall rise above the wider horizon, then what frozen symmetry would not turn into liquid melody? And who among you would not be the cup-bearer to the myrtle and the laurel?

فأجاب قائلاً:

"عندما بين المروج والكروم الناعسة يطل الربيع باحثاً عن الحبيب، ستذوب الثلوج في الوادي سواقي تَنْهَر إلى الغدير ، لتكون حامل الكأس إلى الآس والرند.

"كل الأشياء ستذوب وتغدو أغنياتٍ عندما يأتي الربيع. حتى النجوم، نُدَفُ الثلج الكبرى– تسّاقط على الحقول الأكبرِ الهوينى، ستذوب سواقي تترقرق في نشيد. عندما في الأفق الأرحب تطلع شمس وجهه، فأي نسق جامد لن يذوب ويجري في نشيد؟ وهل بينكم من لا يريد أن يكون حامل الكأس إلى الآس والرند؟

"So shall the snow of your heart melt when your Spring is come, and thus shall your secret run in streams to seek the river of life in the valley. And the river shall enfold your secret and carry it to the great sea.

"It was but yesterday that you were moving with the moving sea, and you were shoreless and without a self. Then the wind, the breath of Life, wove you, a veil of light on her face; then her hand gathered you and gave you form, and with a head held high you sought the heights. But the sea followed after you, and her song is still with you. And though you have forgotten her parentage, she will forever assert her motherhood and forever will she call you unto her.

"It is the snow-flake in you running down to the sea.

"هكذا سيذوب ثلج قلبك حين ربيعك يأتي، وهكذا سيترقرق سرك سواقي تبحث في الوادي عن نهر الوجود. وسوف يحضن النهر سرك ويمضي به إلى البحر الكبير.

"بالأمس فقط، كنتَ مع البحر المائج تموج، بلا شاطئٍ ولا ذات. ثم نسجتك الريح، أنفاس الحياة، على وجهها يَشْمَقَ نور؛ ثم جمعتك يدها وأعطتك شكلاً، فرُحتَ رافعَ الرأس تروم النجود. لكن البحر ظل في إثرِك، وأغنيته لاتزال معك. ورغم أنك نسيت نسَبَك، فلن يألُ يؤكد أبوّتَهُ، وللأبد يناديك إلى أديمه.

"إنها نُدفَةُ الثلجِ فيك تترقرق إلى المحيط."

"In your wanderings among the mountains and the desert you will always remember the depth of her cool heart. And though oftentimes you will not know for what you long, it is indeed for her vast and rhythmic peace.

"And how else can it be? In grove and in bower when the rain dances in leaves upon the hill, when snow falls, a blessing and a covenant; in the valley when you lead your flocks to the river; in your fields where brooks, like silver streams join together the green garment; in your gardens when the early dews mirror the heavens; in your meadows when the mist of evening half veils your way; in all these the sea is with you, a witness to your heritage, and a claim upon your love."

"في تيهك وأنت بين الجبال والصحراء تجول سيطالعك عمق قلبه الندي. ورغم أنك، في الغالب، لن تدرك كنه شوقك، فما شوقك في الحقيقة إلا لإيقاع سلامه الوسيع.

"وكيف يكون الأمر غير ذلك؟ في العرائش والخمائل، والمطر يرقص في الأوراق على الأيك، ويهُرُّ الثلج، بَركةً وعهداً؛ وفي الوادي وأنت تسوق إلى الغدير القطيع؛ وفي الحقولِ والجداولُ سواقي فضة تربط ما بين سندس الأديم؛ وفي الحدائق والصبح ندى يعكس كالمرآة الملكوت؛ وفي المروج وغبَش المساء يحجب أو يكاد الدروب؛ في كل ذلك يكون البحر معك، شاهداً على إرثِك، ودعوىً تطالب بحبك."

And on a morning as they walked in the Garden, there appeared before the gate a woman, and it was Karima, she whom Almustafa loved even as a sister in his boyhood. And she stood without, asking nothing, nor knocking with her hand upon the gate, but only gazing with longing and sadness into the Garden.

And Almustafa saw the desire upon her eyelids, and with swift steps he came to the wall and the gate and opened unto her, and she came in and was made welcome.

And she spoke and said:

"Where have you withdrawn yourself from us altogether, that we may not live in the light of your countenance? For behold, these many years have we loved you and waited with longing for your safe return.

وفيما كانوا يطوفون في الحديقة ذات صباح، ظهرت قبالة البوابة امرأة، وكانت كريمة التي أحبها المصطفى صبياً حب أخ لأخته. وقفت خارج السور، لا تطلب شيئاً، ولا تطرق بيدها الباب، ترنو إلى الحديقة فقط بشوق وحزن.

رأى المصطفى الشوق على جفنيها، فسارع وفتح الباب لها فدخلت يسبقها الترحاب.

وتكلمت وقالت:

"أين غيبت ظلك عنا، وحرمتنا من نور *بهاك؟* طوال تلك السنين أحببناك وانتظرنا عودتك سالماً باشتياق.

"And now the people cry for you and would have speech with you; and I am their messenger come to beseech you that you will show yourself to the people, and speak to them out of your wisdom, and comfort the broken of heart and instruct our foolishness."

And looking upon her, he said:

"Call me not wise unless you call all men wise. A young fruit am I, still clinging to the branch, and it was only yesterday that I was but a blossom.

"And call none among you foolish, for in truth we are neither wise nor foolish. We are green leaves upon the tree of life, and life itself is beyond wisdom, and surely beyond foolishness.

"الناس تلهج باسمك الآن وتريد أن تبادلك الكلام؛ أنا رسولتهم إليك جئت ألتمس خروجك إليهم، فتخاطبهم ومن معين حكمتك تكلمهم، فتواسي كسير القلب وترشدَ فينا الغباوة."

قال لها وعيناه تصافحان عينيها:

"لا تصفيني بالحكيم حتى تصفي كل الرجال بالحكمة. ما أنا إلا ثمرة نابتة، لاتزال تتشبث بغصنها، وكنت للتَو برعماً.

"ولا تصفي بالغباوة أحداً، فنحن لسنا في الحقيقة بحكماء ولا بأغبياء، بل أوراق خضراء على شجرة الحياة، والحياة ذاتها أبعد من الحكمة، ولا شك أبعد من الغباء.

"And have I indeed withdrawn myself from you? Know you not that there is no distance save that which the soul does not span in fancy? And when the soul shall span that distance, it becomes a rhythm in the soul.

"The distance that lies between you and your near neighbour un-befriended is indeed greater than that which lies between you and your beloved who dwells beyond seven lands and seven seas.

"For in remembrances there are no distances; and only in oblivion is there a gulf that neither your voice nor your eye can abridge.

"Between the shores of the ocean and the summit of the highest mountain there is a secret road which you must needs travel ere you become one with the sons of earth.

"وهل نأيت بنفسي حقاً عنكم؟ ألا تعلمين أنْ لا مسافة هناك غير التي لا تقطعها الروح في الخيال؟ وعندما تقطع الروح تلك المسافة، تصبح في الروح إيقاعَ انسجام.

"المسافة التي بينكِ وبين جار جافيتِه لأبعد من التي بينك وبين حبيب لك يقيم خلف سبعةِ بَرارٍ وسبعةِ بحار.

"في الذكريات لا توجد مسافات؛ في النسيان فقط هناك فج لا يستطيع صوتك ولا عينك أن يوجزاه.

"بين شطآن المحيط وقمة أعلى جبل هناك طريق سرية عليك أن تقطعيها قبل أن تصبحي واحدة مع أبناء الأرض.

"And between your knowledge and your understanding there is a secret path which you must need discover ere you become one with man, and therefore one with yourself.

"Between your right hand that gives and your left hand that receives there is a great space. Only by deeming them both giving and receiving can you bring them into spacelessness, for it is only in knowing that you have naught to give and naught to receive that you can overcome the space.

"Verily the vastest distance is that which lies between your sleep-vision and your wakefulness; and between that which is but a deed and that which is a desire.

"وبين معرفتك وفهمك هناك درب سرية لا بد أن تكتشفيها قبل أن تصبحي واحدة مع الإنسان، ومِن ثَمَّ مع نفسك.

"بين يمناك التي تعطي ويسراك التي تتلقى مسافةٌ كبرى لا تلغى حتى ترَينَ أن كليهما تعطي وأن كليهما تتلقى؛ فلن تذللي المسافة قبل أن تدركي أنك لا تملكين ما تعطين وأنك لا تملكين ما تتلقين.

"أكبر المسافات لا مراء هي التي بين رؤيا منامك ويقظتك؛ وبين ما هو فعل وما هو رغبة.

"And there is still another road which you must needs travel ere you become one with Life. But of that road I shall not speak now, seeing that you are weary already of travelling."

Then he went forth with the woman, he and the nine, even unto the market-place, and he spoke to the people, his friends and his neighbours, and there was joy in their hearts and upon their eyelids.

And he said:

"You grow in sleep, and live your fuller life in dreaming. For all your days are spent in thanksgiving for that which you have received in the stillness of the night.

"وهناك طريق أخرى عليك أن تقطعيها قبل أن تصبحي واحدة مع الحياة، لن أتكلم الآن عنها، فأنت متعبة من وعثاء المسير إلى هنا."

ويمم شطر السوق مع المرأة والرجال التسعة، وكلم الناس، أصدقاءه وجيرانه، وماج في قلوبهم تثنى على جفونهم.

وتكلم وقال:

"في النومْ ينمو عودُكم، وفي الحلمْ تعيشون الحياة الأكمل. فكل أيامكم تمضي في شكر على ما نابكم في الليل السَكون.

"Oftentimes you think and speak of night as the season of rest, yet in truth night is the season of seeking and finding.

"The day gives unto you the power of knowledge and teaches your fingers to become versed in the art of receiving but it is night that leads you to the treasure-house of Life.

"The sun teaches to all things that grow their longing for the light but it is night that raises them to the stars.

"It is indeed the stillness of the night that weaves a wedding-veil over the trees in the forest, and the flowers in the garden, and then spreads the lavish feast and makes ready the nuptial chamber; and in that holy silence tomorrow is conceived in the womb of time.

"تحسَبون الليل أوانَ راحة وكأوانٍ راحةٍ تتحدثون عنه، إنما الليل أوان بحث وكشف.

"يمدكم النهار بقوة المعرفة ويعلِّم أصابعَكم فن الأخذ لكنه الليل ما يقودكم إلى الكنوز.

"تعلِّم الشمسُ كلَ ما ينمو شوقَه للنور لكن الليل يعليه إلى النجوم.

"سكون الليل ينسج على أشجار الغابة، وأزهار الحديقة خمارَ العروس، ويمد المائدةَ العامرةَ ويجهزُ المخدعَ الزوجي؛ وفي ذلك الصمت القدسي يتخلّق الغد في رحِم الوقت.

"Thus it is with you, and thus, in seeking, you find meat and fulfilment. And though at dawn your awakening erases the memory, the board of dreams is forever spread and the nuptial chamber waiting."

And he was silent for a space, and they also, awaiting his word. Then he spoke again, saying:

"You are spirits though you move in bodies; and like oil that burns in the dark you are flames though held on lamps.

"هكذا الحال معكم، وهكذا، في البحث، تجدون الزادَ والمُراد. ورغم أن ذاكرتكم يمحوها في الفجر صحوكم، إلا أن مائدة الأحلام تبقى عامرةً وفي الانتظار يبقى المخدع الزوجي."

وصمت برهة، وهم صمتوا، بانتظار كلامه. ثم تكلم ثانية، فقال:

"أنتم أرواح رغم أنكم تتحركون في أجساد؛ ومثل الزيت يحترق في الظلام أنتم لهب رغم أنكم تقومون على مصباح.

"If you were naught save bodies, then my standing before you and speaking unto you would be but emptiness, even as the dead calling unto the dead. But this is not so. All that is deathless in you is free unto the day and the night and cannot be housed or fettered, for this is the will of the Most High. You are His breath even as the wind that shall be neither caught nor caged. And I also am the breath of His breath."

And he went from their midst walking swiftly and entered again into the Garden.

And Sarkis, he who was the half-doubter, spoke and said:

"And what of ugliness, Master? You speak never of ugliness."

"لو كنتم أجساداً ولا شيء غير أجساد، لكان وقوفي أمامكم وحديثي إليكم الآن خَواء، كميت نادى على الأموات. لكن الأمر غير ذلك. ما هو أزلي فيكم حر لليل والنهار لا يعيقه قيد ولا يحيطه جدار، هكذا العليّ شاء. أنتم أنفاسُه، وكالريح أنتم لا يقبضها قابض ولا يطوّقها سوار. وأنا أيضاً فوحُ أنفاسِه."

ومشى عنهم بخطى حثيثة ودخل الحديقة ثانية.

وتكلم مَخّول، الذي يخامره الشك، وقال:

"ماذا عن البشاعة، يا سيدي؟ أنت لا تأتي على ذكر البشاعة أبداً."

And Almustafa answered him, and there was a whip in his voice, and he said:

"My friend, what man shall call you inhospitable if he shall pass by your house, yet would not knock at your door?

"And who shall deem you deaf and unmindful if he shall speak to you in a strange tongue of which you understand nothing?

"Is it not that which you have never striven to reach, into whose heart you have never desired to enter, that you deem ugliness?

"If ugliness is aught, indeed, it is but the scales upon our eyes, and the wax filling our ears.

"Call nothing ugly, my friend, save the fear of a soul in the presence of its own memories."

أجابه المصطفى بنبرة كصَبّ السَوط، وقال:

"يا صديقي، من سيقول إنك غير مِضياف إن مر ببيتك ولم يطرق بابك؟

"ومن سيقول إنك أصم وغير آبه إن حدثك بلسان لم تفهم منه شيئاً؟

"أليس مَن لم تسعَ إليه وصولاً، ورغبت عن دخول قلبه يوماً، هو ما تسميه بشاعة؟

"إذا كان في البشاعة ما يقال، فما البشاعة، وقول الحق، إلا الموازين تُثقِل عيوننا، والشمع يَقِرُ آذاننا.

"لا تتعت بالبشاعة، يا صديقي، شيئاً، اللهم إلا خوفَ روح في حضرة ذكرياتها."

And upon a day as they sat in the long shadows of the white poplars, one spoke saying:

"Master, I am afraid of time. It passes over us and robs us of our youth, and what does it give in return?"

And he answered and said:

"Take up now a handful of good earth. Do you "find in it a seed, and perhaps a worm? If your hand were spacious and enduring enough, the seed might become a forest, and the worm a flock of angels. And forget not that the years which turn seeds to forests, and worms to angels, belong to this *Now*, all of the years, this very *Now*.

في يوم كانوا فيه جالسين في ظلال الحَور الأبيض الممتدة في استطالة، تكلم أحدهم قائلاً:

"أخشى الزمن، ياسيدي. يمر علينا ويسرق الشباب منا، وماذا، حلفتك، يقدم بالمقابل لنا؟"

فأجابه، وقال:

"خذ حفنة من ثرى أرض طيبة. هل تجد فيها بذرة، وربما دودة؟ لو كانت كفك رحبة وذات احتمال، فلربما تصبح البذرة غابة، والدودة سربَ ملائكة. ولا تنس أن السنين التي تحيل البذور غابات، والدود ملائكة، تعود إلى هذا *الآن*، كل السنين، إلى عين هذا *الآن*.

"And what are the seasons of the years save your own thoughts changing? Spring is an awakening in your breast, and summer but a recognition of your own fruitfulness. Is not autumn the ancient in you singing a lullaby to that which is still a child in your being? And what, I ask you, is winter save sleep big with the dreams of all the other seasons?"

And then Mannus, the inquisitive disciple, looked about him and he saw plants in flower cleaving unto the sycamore-tree. And he said:

"Behold the parasites, Master. What say you of them? They are thieves with weary eyelids who steal the light from the steadfast children of the sun, and make fair of the sap that runneth into their branches and their leaves."

"وماذا عسى الفصولَ أن تكونَ غيرَ أفكارك في تبدلها؟ الربيع صحوٌ بصدرك، والصيف اعتراف بخصبك. والخريفُ، أليس الخريفُ قديمَك يهدهد للذي مازال فيك طفلاً؟ وماذا، سألتك، عسى الشتاءَ أن يكونَ غيرَ نوم كبُرَ بأحلام الفصول الأخرى؟"

ونظر عاصي، الرجل السؤول، حوله ورأى إلى نباتات قد أينعت ومالت على شجرة الجمّيز. رأى وقال:

"أيها المعلم، انظرِ الطفيليات. ماذا تقول فيها؟ إنها لصوص بأجفان مثقَّلة تسلب النور من الصامدين من أبناء الشمس، وتستبيح نسغه الجاري في أغصانها وأوراقها."

And he answered him saying:

"My friend, we are all parasites. We who labour to turn the sod into pulsing life are not above those who receive life directly from the sod without knowing the sod.

"Shall a mother say to her child: 'I give you back to the forest, which is your greater mother, for you weary me, heart and hand?'

"Or shall the singer rebuke his own song, saying: 'Return now to the cave of echoes from whence you came, for your voice consume my breath?'

"And shall the shepherd say to the yearling: 'I have no pasture whereunto I may lead you; therefore be cut off and become a sacrifice for this cause?'

فأجابه قائلاً:

"كلنا طفيليات، يا صديقي. نحن الذين نكِد لنحيل المرج روضاً ينبِض بالحياة لا نزيد عمن يستمد من المرج الحياة غيرَ عالِم بالمرج.

"هل تقول أمٌ لطفلها: 'أعيدك إلى الغابة، أمِك الكبرى، أنت تتعبني، قلباً ويدا؟'

"هل ينتهر الأغنية من يغنيها، قائلاً لها: 'عودي إلى كهف الصدى الذي منه أتيت، صُواتُك يستنفد أنفاسي؟'

"هل يقول الراعي للحمَل: 'لا مرعى أقودك إليه؛ فانبَتِر وكن لهذا السببِ ضحية؟'

"Nay, my friend, all these things are answered even before they are asked, and, like your dreams, are fulfilled ere you sleep.

"We live upon one another according to the law, ancient and timeless. Let us live thus in loving-kindness. We seek one another in our aloneness, and we walk the road when we have no hearth to sit beside.

"My friends and my brothers, the wider road is your fellow-man.

"These plants that live upon the tree draw milk of the earth in the sweet stillness of night, and the earth in her tranquil dreaming sucks at the breast of the sun.

"لا، يا صديقي، هذه أشياء تُجاب قبل أن تُسأل، ومثلُ أحلامك، تتحقق قبل أن تنام.

"بعضنا يعيش على بعض حسب القانون– قديم وأزلي. فلنحيا بود قَوامُه محبة. ويسعى بعضنا إلى بعض إذ تحاصرنا الوحدة، وعندما لا يكون هناك موقد نجلس بجانبه نلوذ بالطريق.

"يا أصدقائي وإخوتي، الطريق الأرحب هو رفيقكم الإنسان.

"هذه النباتات التي تقتات على الشجرة تمتص حليب الأرض في عليل الليل، وفي أحلامها المطمئنة ترضَع الأرضُ من ثدي الشمس.

"And the sun, even as you and I and all there is, sits in equal honour at the banquet of the Prince whose door is always open and whose board is always spread.

"Mannus, my friend, all there is lives always upon all there is; and all there is lives in the faith, shoreless, upon the bounty of the Most High."

And on a morning when the sky was yet pale with dawn, they walked altogether in the Garden and looked unto the East and were silent in the presence of the rising sun.

And after a while Almustafa pointed with his hand, and he said: 'The image of the morning sun in a dewdrop is not less than the sun. The reflection of life in your soul is not less than Life.

"والشمس، مثلي ومثلَك ومثلَ كلِ حي، تجلس على مائدة الأمير بتشريفٍ سَواء، هذا الذي بابه مشرع وسفرته عامرةٌ في النهار والليل.

"عاصي، يا صديقي، كل حي يعيش على كل حي؛ وكل حي، بلا شاطئ، يعيش في الإيمان على أجر العلِي."

ذات صباح والسماء موشاة بشحوب الفجر، طافوا في الحديقة وأبصارهم شاخصة للشرق وفي حضرة الشمس الطالعة استبدهم الصمت.

بعد هنيهة أشار المصطفى بيده، وقال:

"تصويرة شمس الصباح في قطرة الندى ليست بأقل من الشمس. استبصار الحياة في روحك ليس بأقل من الحياة.

"The dewdrop mirrors the light because it is one with light, and you reflect life because you and Life are one.

"When darkness is upon you, say: 'This darkness is dawn not yet born; and though night's travail be full upon me, yet dawn shall be born unto me even as unto the hills.'

"The dewdrop rounding its sphere in the dusk of the lily is not unlike yourself gathering your soul in the heart of God.

"Shall a dewdrop say: 'But once in a thousand years I am even a dewdrop,' speak you and answer it saying: 'Know you not that the light of all the years is shining in your circle?'"

"قطرة الندى تعكس النورَ لأنها والنورَ واحد، وتعكس أنت الحياة لأنك والحياةَ واحد.

"عندما تغشاك الظلمة، قل: 'هذا الظلام فجر لم يولد بعد؛ ورغم أن مخاض الليل حولي في ذروته، فلسوف يطلع الفجرُ عليَّ طلوعَه على التلال.'

"قطرة الندى تتكور في غسق الزنبقِ، لا تختلف عنك وأنت تستجمِع روحَكَ في قلب الله.

"هَبْ أن قطرة ندى قالت: 'إنما أنا قطرة ندى مرة كل ألف عام،' فتكلم وأجبها وقل لها: 'أما علمت أن نور السنين كلَها يشع في سماكِ؟'"

And on an evening a great storm visited the place, and Almustafa and his disciples, the nine, went within and sat about the fire and were silent.

Then one of the disciples said:

"I am alone, Master, and the hoofs of the hours beat heavily upon my breast."

And Almustafa rose up and stood in their midst, and he said in a voice like unto the sound of a great wind:

"Alone! And what of it. You came alone, and alone shall you pass into the mist.

"Therefore drink your cup alone and in silence. The autumn days have given other lips other cups and filled them with wine bitter and sweet, even as they have filled your cup.

ذات مساء زارتِ المكانَ عاصفة هوجاء، فدخل المصطفى والتسعة البيت وجلسوا صامتين حول النار.

نظر أحد تلامذته إليه وقال:

"سيدي، إني وحيد، وحوافر الساعات تُثخِن في صدري."

نهض المصطفى وتوسط الجمع، وقال بصوت كعصف ريح:

"وحيد! ما بها؟ جئت وحيداً، وستمضي في الضباب وأنت وحيد.

"فارشف كأسك لوحدك وارشفها في سُكات. أيام الخريف أعطت شفاهً أخرى كؤوساً أخرى وأترعتها بمر وحلو النبيذ، مثلما أترعَت كأسك.

77

"Drink your cup alone though it tastes of your own blood and tears, and praise life for the gift of thirst. For without thirst your heart is but the shore of a barren sea, songless and without a tide.

"Drink your cup alone, and drink it with cheers.

"Raise it high above your head and drink deep to those who drink alone.

"Once I sought the company of men and sat with them at their banquet-tables and drank deep with them; but their wine did not rise to my head, nor did it flow into my bosom. It only descended to my feet. My wisdom was left dry and my heart was locked and sealed. Only my feet were with them in their fog.

"And I sought the company of men no more, nor drank wine with them at their board.

"ارشف كأسك لوحدك ولو كانت من مذاق الدم والدموع، وهلِّل للحياة على نعمة الظمأ. فما قلبك إلا شاطئٌ بلا ماءٍ، ولا أغنياتٍ ولا مَدٍ وجَزرٍ لولا الظمأ.

"إشرب كأسك لوحدك. واشربها في ابتهاج.

"ارفعها عالياً فوق رأسك واشرب نخب الشاربين في انفراد.

"لقد كان أني سعيت إلى صحبة رجال جلست على موائدهم وشربت معهم؛ لكن خمرتهم لم تصعد لرأسي، ولم تتسرِب لصدري. نزلت إلى قدمَي. وبقيت حكمتي مجدِبةً وقلبي أُغلِق وخُتِم عليه. في غباشتهم لم أكن معهم إلا بقدمَي.

"ولم أسعَ لصحبة الرجال بعد ذلك قط، ولم أحتس النبيذ معهم على موائدهم.

"Therefore I say unto you, though the hoofs of the hours beat heavily upon your bosom, what of it? It is well for you to drink your cup of sorrow alone, and your cup of joy shall you drink also."

And on a day, as Phaedrus, the Greek, walked in the Garden, he struck his foot upon a stone and he was angered. And he turned and picked up the stone, saying in a low voice: 'O dead thing in my path!' and he flung away the stone.

And Almustafa, the chosen and the beloved, said: "Why say you 'O dead thing?' Have you been thus long in this Garden and know not that there is nothing dead here? All things live and glow in the knowledge of the day and the majesty of the night. You and the stone are one. There is a difference only in heart-beats. Your heart beats a little faster, does it, my friend? Ay, but it is not so tranquil.

"لهذا أقول لك- رغم إمعان حوافر الساعات دَوساً في صدرك، ما بها؟ إشرب كأس حزنك لوحدك، وكأسَ فرحك ستشربها أيضاً."

كان فيلمون، اليوناني، يتمشى في الحديقة ذات يوم فعثرت قدمه بحجر فاغتاظ فاستدار فالتقط الحجر، وتمتم: 'لم يبق إلا هذا الشيء الميت لأعثر به!' وهوى بالحجر.

فقال المصطفى، المختار الحبيب:

"لماذا تقول 'هذا الشيء الميت؟' أمضيتَ زمناً في هذه الحديقة ولا تعلم أنْ لا شيءَ ميتٌ هنا؟ كل الأشياء تتنفس وتتوهج بعلم النهار وجلال الليل. أنت والحجر واحد. لا فرق بينكما إلا بدقات القلب. قلبُك يخفق أسرع قليلاً، أليس كذلك، يا صديقي؟ أجل، لكن ليس بالاطمئنان ذاتِه.

"Its rhythm may be another rhythm, but I say unto you that if you sound the depths of your soul and scale the heights of space, you shall hear one melody, and in that melody the stone and the star sing, the one with the other, in perfect unison.

"If my words reach not your understanding, then let it be until another dawn. If you have cursed this stone because in your blindness you have stumbled upon it, then would you curse a star if so be your head should encounter it in the sky? But the day will come when you gather stones and stars as a child plucks the valley-lilies, and then shall you know that all these are living and fragrant."

"ربما كان إيقاعُه مختلفاً، لكن إن سبرت أعماقَ روحِكِ واختبرت أعالي الفضاء، فلسوف تسمع ترنيمة واحدة، يغني فيها الحجر والنجم، كل مع الآخرِ، بكامل انسجام.

"إن لم تصل كلماتي فهمك، فدع إلى غير فجر. إن أنت لعنتَ هذا الحجر لأنك في عماك عثُرت به، فهل ستلعن نجماً يرتطم رأسك به في السماء؟ لكنّ يوماً سيأتي تلقُط فيه حجارة ونجوماً كما يلقُط طفلٌ زنابق الوادي، وحينها ستدرك أن هذه تعبق بالشذى وتمور بالحياة."

And on the first day of the week when the sounds of the temple bells sought their ears, one spoke and said:

"Master, we hear much talk of God hereabout. What say you of God, and who is He in very truth?"

And he stood before them like a young tree, fearless of wind or tempest, and he answered saying:

"Think now, my comrades and beloved, of a heart that contains all your hearts, a love that encompasses all your loves, a spirit that envelops all your spirits, a voice enfolding all your voices, and a silence deeper than all your silences, and timeless.

في اليوم الأول من أيام الأسبوع ورنين أجراس المعبد يتهادى إلى الأسماع، تكلم أحدهم وقال:

"أيها المعلم، نسمع كثيراً عن الله هنا وهناك. ما قولك في الله، ومن في الحقيقة الحقةِ يكون؟"

وقف كشجرة يافعة، لا تبالي بريح أو إعصار، وقال:

"يا رفاقي وأحبتي، فكروا بقلب يضم كل قلوبكم، وبحب يختزن كل ماعرفتموه من حب، وبروح تعانق كلَ أرواحِكم، وبصوت يُرجِع كلَ أصواتِكم، وبصمت أعمقَ من كل سكَناتِكم، وأزلي.

"Seek now to perceive in your self-fullness a beauty more enchanting than all things beautiful, a song more vast than the songs of the sea and the forest, a majesty seated upon the throne for which Orion is but a footstool, holding a sceptre in which the Pleiades are naught save the glimmer of dewdrops.

"And if my words are a rock and a riddle, then seek, none the less, that your hearts may be broken, and that your questionings may bring you unto the love and the wisdom of the Most High, whom men call God."

"آنِسوا الآنَ وبمَلء شغافكم أن تُبصِروا جمالاً أكثر بهاء من كل جميل، أغنيةً أكبَرَ من أغنيات الغاب والبحر، جلالاً يعتلي عرشاً ما بُرجُ الجوزاءِ لكرسيّه إلا مسندُ قدمين، يمتشق صولجاناً ما نجوم الثُّريا في نمنماته إلا ندىً يومض في ليل.

"إذا كانت هذي كلماتي جُلموداً ولُغزاً، فلا تألوا رغم هذا أن تتكسر قلوبكم، وتأخذَكم الأسئلةُ إلى حب وحكمة العلي، الذي يسميه الأنامُ الله."

And they were silent, every one, and they were perplexed in their heart; and Almustafa was moved with compassion for them, and he gazed with tenderness upon them and said:

"Let us speak no more now of God the Father. Let us speak rather of the gods, your neighbours, and of your brothers, the elements that move about your houses and your fields.

"You would rise up in fancy unto the cloud, and you would deem it height; and you would pass over the vast sea and claim it to be distance. But I say unto you that when you sow a seed in the earth, you reach a greater height; and when you hail the beauty of the morning to your neighbour, you cross a greater sea.

وصمتوا، كلهم صمتوا، وحارت قلوبهم؛ وغمر المصطفى عطف عليهم، وفي عطفه رنا إليهم وقال:

"كفانا حديثاً عن الله الأب. ولنتحدث عن الأرباب، جيرانكم، وعن أشقائكم، العناصرِ التي تتحرك حول بيوتكم وحقولكم.

"تصعدون بالخيال إلى السحاب وتحسَبون السحابَ أوجاً؛ وتعبرون البحر الواسع وتظننون البحرَ بَوناً. وأقول لكم إنكم إذ تزرعون بذرةً، تبلغون أوجاً أعظم؛ وإذ تهللون لجمال الصباح تحيّون به جاركم، تعبرون بحراً أعظم.

"Too often do you sing God, the infinite, and yet in truth you hear not the song. Would that you might listen to the song-birds, and to the leaves that forsake the branch when the wind passes by, and forget not, my friends, that these sing only when they are separated from the branch!

"Again I bid you to speak not so freely of God, who is your All, but speak rather and understand one another, neighbour unto neighbour, a god unto a god.

"For what shall feed the fledgling in the nest if the mother bird flies skyward? And what anemone in the fields shall be fulfilled unless it be husbanded by a bee from another anemone?

"كثيراً ما تُنشِدون الله، الذي بلا بداية ولا نهاية، ولا تسمعون في الحقيقة الغناء. ليتكم تصغون للطير المغرد، وللأوراق تهجر الغصن مع كل هبة ريح، ولا تنسوا، يا أصدقائي، أن هذه لا تغني إلا عندما تهجر الغصن!

"أحلفكم من جديد، لا تتحدثوا بحرية هكذا عن الله، وهو كلُ ما أنتم، وليتحدث بعضكم إلى بعض وليفهم بعضكم بعضاً، جار وجار، إله وإله.

"فمن سيطعِم فراخ العش إذا صفقت أمها الجناح وكانت وِجهتُها السماء؟ وأيُ زهرةٍ حمراء مبقعةٌ بنقاط سوداء ستجد الاكتفاء إن لم ترعَها نحلةٌ من شقيقة أخرى بين شقائق النعمان؟

"It is only when you are lost in your smaller selves that you seek the sky which you call God. Would that you might find paths into your vast selves; would that you might be less idle and pave the roads!

"My mariners and my friends, it were wiser to speak less of God, whom we cannot understand, and more of each other, whom we may understand. Yet I would have you know that we are the breath and the fragrance of God. We are God, in leaf, in flower, and oftentimes in fruit."

"في تيهكم داخلَ ذواتِكمُ الصغرى تبتهلون إلى السماء التي تسمونها الله. ليتكم تجدون إلى ذواتكم الكبرى دروباً؛ وتكونون في تمهيدها أقلَ توانياً!

"يا بحارتي ويا أصدقائي، تقضي الحكمة أن نقلل من الحديث عن الله، الذي لا نفهم، وأن نكثِر من الحديث عن بعضِنا بعضاً، فقد يفهم بعضُنا بعضاً. ولتعلموا أننا نفحُ وعطرُ الله. نحن الله، في الورقة، وفي الزهرة، وغالباً في الثمَرة، نحن الله."

AND on a morning when the sun was high, one of the disciples, one of those three who had played with him in childhood, approached him saying:

"Master, my garment is worn and I have no other. Give me leave to go unto the market-place and bargain that perchance I may procure me new raiment."

And Almustafa looked upon the young man, and he said: 'Give me your garment.' And he did so and stood naked in the noonday.

And Almustafa said in a voice that was like a steed running upon a road:

"Only the naked live in the sun. Only the artless ride the wind. And he alone who loses his way a thousand times shall have a home-coming.

ذات صباح والشمس في غرة السماء، اقترب أحد الذين لعبوا معه طفلاً، وقال:

"سيدي، حُلتي بالية ولا أملك غيرها. أستأذنك بالذهاب إلى السوق أساوم فيها، لعلي أبتاع حلة جديدة."

نظر المصطفى إلى الشاب، وقال: 'هاتِ حلتك.'

فأعطاه الشاب حلته وبقي تحت شمس الظهيرة بلا رداء.

فقال المصطفى بصوت كعَدْو جواد:

"وحده العاري الحاسر يعيش في الشمس. وحده الغِر البريء يركب الريح. والذي يضيّع طريقه ألف مرة وحده سينعم بعودة إلى بيته القديم.

"The angels are tired of the clever. And it was but yesterday that an angel said to me: 'We created hell for those who glitter. What else but fire can erase a shining surface and melt a thing to its core?'

And I said: "But in creating hell you created devils to govern hell." But the angel answered: 'Nay, hell is governed by those who do not yield to fire.'

"Wise angel! He knows the ways of men and the ways of half men. He is one of the seraphim who come to minister unto the prophets when they are tempted by the clever. And no doubt he smiles when the prophets smile, and weeps also when they weep.

"الملائكة أتعبها الألمعي. بالأمس فقط قال لي ملاك:
'خلَقنا الجحيم لمن يبرِقون. ماذا غير النار ما يبيد ظاهراً
يسطع ويذيب الشيء عن بَكرة أبيه؟'

"فقلت: 'خلقتُم الجحيمَ وأوجدتم شياطينَ لتحكم الجحيم.'
فأجابني الملاك: 'كلا، الجحيم يحكمه الذين لا يطالهم
السعير.'

"يا للملاك الحكيم! يعرف طرق الرجال وطرُق أنصاف
الرجال. هو من ملائكة السيرافيم الذين يوحون للأنبياء عندما
يغويهم الألمعي. ويبتسم لا شك حين يبتسم الأنبياء، ويبكي
أيضاً عندما يبكون.

"My friends and my mariners, only the naked live in the sun. Only the rudderless can sail the greater sea. Only he who is dark with the night shall wake with the dawn, and only he who sleeps with the roots under the snow shall reach the spring.

"For you are even like roots, and like roots are you simple, yet you have wisdom from the earth. And you are silent, yet you have within your unborn branches the choir of the four winds.

"You are frail and you are formless, yet you are the beginning of the giant oaks, and of the half-pencilled pattern of the willows against the sky.

"يا أصدقائي ويا بحارتي، وحده العاري يعيش في الشمس. ومن كان بلا دفة وحده يركب البحر الكبير. ومن قاسم الليل حلكته وحده سيصحو مع الفجر، ومن نام تحت غطاء الثلج مع الجذور وحده سيدرك الربيع.

"فأنتم مثل الجذور، وبسطاء مثل الجذور، لكن فيكم حكمة من الأرض. وأنتم صامتون، لكن جوقة الرياح الأربع تتنفس في فروعكم التي لم تولد بعد.

"أنتم واهنون وأنتم بلا شكل، لكنكم انبثاق السنديان الأشم، ومشق الصفصاف على بيرق الغيم.

"Once more I say, you are but roots betwixt the dark and the moving heavens. And oftentimes have I seen you rising to dance with the light, but I have also seen you shy. All roots are shy. They have hidden their hearts so long that they know not what to do with their hearts.

"But May shall come, and May is a restless virgin, and she shall mother the hills and plains."

AND one who has served in the Temple besought him saying:

"Teach us, Master, that our words may be even as your words, a chant and an incense unto the people."

"أعيد بعد أن قلت، ما أنتم إلا جذور بين السماوات الظلماء والسابحة في الفُلك. ولكم أبصرتكم تصعدون لتراقصوا النور، لكني أبصرتكم كذلك في حياء. كل الجذور خجول. أخفت قلوبها طويلاً فلم تعد تعرف ماذا تفعل بالقلوب.

"لكن عذراء أيار آتية، عذراء هائجة، وستكون أماً للتلال وللسهول."

وخاطبه أحد الذين خدموا في المعبد مناشداً:

"أيها المعلم، علمنا كيف تتنزِل كلماتُنا على الناس صدحاً وطيباً، مثلَ كلماتك؟"

And Almustafa answered and said:

"You shall rise beyond your words, but your path shall remain, a rhythm and a fragrance; a rhythm for lovers and for all those who are beloved, and a fragrance for those who would live life in a garden.

"But you shall rise beyond your words to a summit whereon the star-dusk falls, and you shall open your hands until they are filled; then you shall lie down and sleep like a white fledgling in a white nest, and shall dream of your tomorrow as white violets dream of spring.

"Ay, and you shall go down deeper than your words. You shall seek the lost fountain-heads of the streams, and you shall be a hidden cave echoing the faint voices of the depths which now you do not even hear.

أجاب المصطفى وقال:

"ستصعد أبعدَ من كلماتك، لكن دربك ستبقى إيقاعاً وشذى؛ إيقاعاً للعاشقين ولكل الذين يحبون ويحبهم الآخرون، وشذى لمن يهوى الحياة في حديقة.

"لكنك ستصعد أبعدَ من كلماتك إلى قمة تغتسل بغسق النجوم، وستفتح يديك حتى تمتلئا؛ فتتمددَ وتنامَ في عش أبيضَ كطير أبيضَ بعدُ لا يطير، وستحلم بغدك مثلما يحلم البنفسج الأبيض بالربيع.

"أجل، وستغوص أعمقَ من كلماتك. وستفتش عن ينابيع الجداول الضائعة، وستكون كهفاً خفية ترجِع صدى أصوات الأعماق الخافتة التي لا تسمعها اليوم.

"You shall go down deeper than your words, ay, deeper than all sounds, to the very heart of the earth, and there you shall be alone with Him who walks also upon the Milky Way."

And after a space one of the disciples asked him saying:

"Master, speak to us of *being*. What is it to *be?*"

"ستغوص أعمق من كلماتك، أجل، أعمق من كل الأصوات، إلى سويداء الأرض، وهناك ستكون لوحدك معه، مع الذي يمشي على المجرة، أمِ النجوم."

وسأله أحدهم قائلاً:

"أيها المعلم، حدثنا عن *الكينونة*. ماذا يعني أن *نكون*؟"

And Almustafa looked long upon him and loved him. And he stood up and walked a distance away from them; then returning, he said:

"In this Garden my father and my mother lie, buried by the hands of the living; and in this Garden lie buried the seeds of yesteryear, brought hither upon the wings of the wind. Athousand times shall my mother and my father be buried here, and a thousand times shall the wind burry the seed; and a thousand years hence shall you and I and these flowers come together in this Garden even as now, and we shall *be*, loving life, and we shall *be*, dreaming of space, and we shall *be*, rising towards the sun.

نظر المصطفى إلى الرجل ورق قلبه له. ثم نهض ومشى؛
وعاد يقول:

"في هذه الحديقة يرقد أبي وترقد أمي، أودعَتهما الثرى
أيدي الأحياء؛ وفي هذه الحديقة دُفِنَت بذورُ ماضي السنين،
نثرتها أجنحة الريح. ألفَ مرة ستُدفَن أمي هنا وسيُدفَن أبي،
وألفَ مرة ستَدفِن البذرةَ الريحِ؛ ولسوف نأتي إلى هذه الحديقة
معاً بعد ذلك بألف عام، أنت وأنا وهذه الزهور كما نحن
اليوم، ولسوف نكونُ، محبين للحياة، ولسوف نكونُ، حالمين
بالفضاء، ولسوف نكونُ، نحو الشمس صاعدين.

"But now today to *be* is to be wise, though not a stranger to the foolish; it is to be strong, but not to the undoing of the weak; to play with young children, not as fathers, but rather as playmates who would learn their games;

"To be simple and guileless with old men and women, and to sit with them in the shade of the ancient oak-trees, though you are still walking with spring;

"To seek a poet though he may live beyond the seven rivers, and to be at peace in his presence, nothing wanting, nothing doubting, and with no question upon your lips;

"والآن اليوم فأن تكونَ يعني أن تكونَ حكيماً، ولا تبدو غريباً على الأرقَع البليد؛ أن تكون قوياً، ولا تحِل عُرى المستضعفين؛ أن تلعب مع الأطفال الصغار، لا كأبٍ، بل كرفيق يريد أن يتعلم كيف يلعبون؛

"أن تكون بسيطاً صادقاً مع المسنين، وتجلس معهم في فَيء السنديان العتيق، حتى وأنت تخطو لا تزال مع الربيع؛

"أن تقصد شاعراً ولو كان خلف الأنهر السبعة، وتشعر بالسلام في وجوده، لا يعوزك شيء، ولا يساورك شك، ولا سؤال يلوح على شفتيك؛

"To know that the saint and the sinner are twin brothers, whose father is our Gracious King, and that one was born but the moment before the other, wherefore we regard him as the Crowned Prince;

"To follow Beauty even when she shall lead you to the verge of the precipice; and though she is winged and you are wingless, and though she shall pass beyond the verge, follow her, for where Beauty is not, there is nothing;

"To be a garden without walls, a vineyard without a guardian, a treasure-house for ever open to passers-by;

"أن تعلم أن القديس والآثم أخَوان توأمان، أبوهما ملكُنا الرحيم، وأن أحدهما وُلِد قبل الآخر بلحظة واحدة، ولهذا ناديناه ولياً للعرش؛

"أن تتبَع الجمال وإن قادك إلى شفا جرف عميق؛ ورغم أنه ذو جناح وأنت بلا جناح، وأنه سيجتاز دونك الجرف، اتبعه، فحيث لا يكون هناك جمال، لا يكون هناك شيء؛

"أن تكون حديقة بلا سور، كرماً بلا ناطر، بيت مال مشرعاً للعابرين؛

"And now, to you also whose hands fashion and find all things that are needful for the comfort of our days and our nights–

"To be robbed, cheated, deceived, ay, misled and trapped and then mocked, yet with it all to look down from the height of your larger self, and smile, knowing that there is spring that will come to your garden to dance in your leaves, and an autumn to ripen your grapes; knowing that if but one of your windows is open to the East, you shall never be empty; knowing that all those deemed wrongdoers and robbers, cheaters and deceivers are your brothers in need, and that you are perchance all of these in the eyes of the blessed inhabitants of that City Invisible, above this city.

"والآن، يا من تصوغ أياديهم وتبصر ما نحتاجه لرغد أيامنا ولیالینا، لكم أيضاً أقول-

"أن يسرقَك الآخرُ، ويغُشَك ويخدعَك-أجل، ويضلِلَك ويتربصَ بك الدوائر ثم يتهكم بك، فترنو من علياء ذاتك الأكبر مبتسماً رغم ذلك، مدركاً أن ربيعاً سيحِل في بستانك ويرقص في أوراقك، وأن خريفاً سيأتي ويُنضِجُ عنبَك؛ ومدركاً أن نافذة واحدة من نوافذِك مشرعةً على الشرق ستأى بك إلى الأبد عن فراغك؛ ومدركاً أن الذين احتُسِبوا لصوصاً وخطائين، وأهلَ خداعٍ وغِشٍ، ما هم إلا إخوة لك في ضيق، وأنك قد تكون كلَ هؤلاء بعين المباركين الساكنين في مدينة الغيب، التي فوق هذه المدينة.

113

"To *be* is to be a weaver with seeing fingers, a builder mindful of light and space; to be a ploughman and feel that you are hiding a treasure with every seed you sow; to be a fisherman and a hunter with a pity for the fish and for the beast, yet a still greater pity for the hunger and need of man.

"And, above all, I say this: I would have you each and everyone partners to the purpose of every man, for only so shall you hope to obtain your own good purpose.

"My comrades and my beloved, be bold and not meek; be spacious and not confined; and until my final hour and yours be indeed your greater self."

"أن تكون يعني أن تكون حائكاً بأصابع مبصرة، بنّاءً يراعي البُعدَ والنور؛ أن تكون حارثاً مع كل بذرة تزرعها تشعر أنك تخبئ كَنزاً؛ أن تكون صياداً يشفق على السمك والطير، وأكثر ما يشفق على جوع وحاجة الإنسان.

"فوق كل هذا، أقول: أتمنى أن تكونوا جميعاً، كل واحد فيكم، شركاء في غاية كل إنسان، فليس غير هذا ما تُآنِسُ به أملَكَ في نَيلِ مُناك.

"يا رفاقي وأحبتي، كونوا المقدام الجسور لا الخنوع الجبان؛ عانقوا المدى ولا ترضَوا بأسر؛ وإلى أن تحين ساعتي وساعتُكم، كونوا ذاتَكم الأكبرَ، بالقول والفعل."

And he ceased from speaking and there fell a deep gloom upon the nine, and their heart was turned away from him, for they understand not his words.

And behold, the three men who were mariners longed for the sea; and they who had served in the Temple yearned for the consolation of her sanctuary; and they who had been his playfellows desired the market-place. They all were deaf to his words, so that the sound of them returned unto him like weary and homeless birds seeking refuge.

And the chosen and the beloved walked a distance from them in the Garden, saying nothing, nor looking upon them.

And they began to reason among themselves, and to seek excuse for their longing to be gone.

وأمسك عن الكلام وحلت قتامة على الرجال حولت القلوب عنه. فلم يفقَه أحد قوله.

ولاحظوا، تاق البحارة الثلاثة إلى البحر ؛ واشتاق سدنة المعبد لسلوى المحراب؛ والذين لعبوا معه طفلاً حنّوا للسوق. كل الآذان وقَرَت عن كلماته التي ارتدت أصواتُها إليه ارتدادَ طيور شريدة أعياها البحث عن ملاذ.

وابتعد المختار الحبيب عنهم ثم وطأ الحديقة، لا يقول شيئاً، ولا ينظر إلى شيء.

وطفَقوا هم يتفكرون كيف يغادرون.

And behold, they turned and went every man to his own place, so that the chosen and the beloved was left alone. And when the night was fully come, he took his steps to the grave-side of his mother and sat beneath the cedar-tree which grew above the place. And there came the shadow of a great light upon the sky, and the Garden shone like a fair jewel upon the breast of earth.

And the chosen and the beloved cried out in the aloneness of his spirit, and he said:

"Heavy-laden is my soul with her own ripe fruit. Who is there would come and take and be satisfied? Is there not one who has fasted and who is kindly and generous in heart to come and break his fast upon my first yieldings to the sunand thus ease me of the weight of my own abundance?

ولا حِظوا، أدار كل منهم ظهره وعاد من حيث أتى تاركاً المختار الحبيب لوحده. وعندما خيم الليل بسواده، أخذته قدماه إلى قبر أمه فجلس تحت الأرز المنيف فوقه. فإذا بظل نور عظيم يضيء السماء، وبالحديقة تتلألأ كجوهرة سطعت على جِيْد الأرض.

في وِحدة روحه، ناح المختار الحبيب، وقال:

"مثقلة روحي بيانع ثمارها. هل مَن يأتي ويأخذُ ويَقِرُّ عيناً؟ ألا من صائمٍ أريحيٍ كريمِ القلب يكسر صيامه على فاتحة غلالي للشمس فيريحني من ثِقَل وَفري؟"

"My soul is running over with the wine of the ages. Is there no thirsty one to come and drink?

"Behold, there was a man standing at the crossroads with hands stretched forth unto the passers-by, and his hands were filled with jewels. And he called upon the passers-by, saying: 'Pity me, and take from me. In God's name take out of my hands and console me.'"

"But the passers-by only looked upon him, and none took out of his hand.

"Would rather that he were a beggar stretching forth his hand to receive – ay, a shivering hand, and brought back empty to his bosom – than to stretch it forth full of rich gifts and find none to receive.

"روحي تفيض بخمرة العصور فهل من ظامئ يأتي ويشرب؟"

"لقد كان أن رجلاً وقف على مفرق طريق ويداه ممدودتان للعابرين، ومليئتان بالحُلي. نادى: 'حِنّوا علي. خذوا مني. حلفتكم باسم العلي أن تأخذوا من يدي مواساة لي.'"

"ولم يكن من العابرين إلا أن نظروا إليه. لم يأخذ أحد شيئاً من يديه.

"ليته كان شحاذاً يمد يداً للصدقات– نعم، يداً مرتعشة، تعود خاوية لصدره، لأفضل من أن يمدها ملأى بثمين الهبات ولا يجد من يأخذ منه.

"And behold, there was also the gracious prince who raised up his silken tents between the mountain and the desert and bade his servants to burn fire, a sign to the stranger and the wanderer; and who sent forth his slaves to watch the road that they might fetch a guest. But the roads and the paths of the desert were unyielding, and they found no one.

"Would rather that prince were a man of nowhere and nowhen, seeking food and shelter. Would that he were the wanderer with naught but his staff and an earthen vessel. For then at nightfall would he meet with his kind, and with the poets of nowhere and nowhen, and share their beggary and their remembrances and their dreaming.

"وكان أيضاً أن أميراً كريماً نصَب بين الجبل والصحراء خيام حرير وأمر بإيقاد النار، علامة للرحالة والغريب؛ وأرسل عبيده لمراقبة الطريق لعلهم يعودون بضيف. لكن طرق ودروب الصحراء كانت حروناً، فلم يجدوا من يعودون به.

"ليت ذاك الأميرَ كان رجلاً من اللازمن واللامكان، يبحث عن طعام وملاذ. ليته كان ذاك الجوّالَ الجوّابَ الذي لا يملك من المتاع إلا عصاً وإناء، فإذا ما حل الليل التقى مع صِنفه، ومع شعراء اللازمن واللامكان، فقاسمهم شحاذتهم وقاسمهم ذكرياتهم وقاسمهم الأحلام.

"And behold, the daughter of the great king rose from sleep and put upon her her silken raiment and her pearls and rubies and she scattered musk upon her hair and dipped her fingers in amber. Then she descended from her tower to her garden, where the dew of night found her golden sandals.

"In the stillness of the night the daughter of the great king sought love in the garden, but in all the vast kingdom of her father there was none who was her lover.

"وكان أن ابنة الملك العظيم نهضت من النوم ولبست ثوبها الحرير وترصعت بالدر والمرجان ورشت شعرها بالمسك وغمست أصابعها بالكهرمان. ثم نزلت من برجها إلى حديقتها، وكشف الندى عن خُفِّها الذهبي.

"في هزيع الليل بحثت ابنة الملك المعظم عن الحب، لكنها في كل مملكة أبيها المترامية لم تجد أيَ حبيب.

"Would rather that she were the daughter of a ploughman, tending his sheep in a field, and returning to her father's house at eventide with the dust of the curving roads upon her feet, and the fragrance of the vineyards in the folds of her raiment. And when the night is come, and the angel of the night is upon the world, she would steal her steps to the river-valley where her lover waits.

"Would that she were a nun in a cloister burning her heart for incense, that her heart may rise to the wind, and exhausting her spirit, a candle, for a light arising toward the greater light, together with all those who worship and those who love and are beloved.

"Would rather that she were a woman ancient of years, sitting in the sun and remembering who had shared her youth."

"ليتها كانت ابنة فلاح، ترعى لأبيها القطيع، وتعود إلى بيته في العشي وعلى قدميها غبار الدروب ومن ثنايا ثوبها يتضوع عبق الكروم. وعندما يأتي المساء، ويطل على الأنام ملاك الليل، تتسلل إلى وادي النهر حيث ينتظرها الحبيب.

"ليتها كانت راهبة في دير تحرق قلبها بَخوراً يَصَّعَد للريح، وتستنزف روحَها، شمعةً، تصَّعَد نوراً يطلُب النورَ الكبير، مع الذين يتعبدون والذين يحبون ويحبهم الآخرون.

"ليتها كانت امرأة غزاها المشيب، تجلس في الشمس وتتذكر الذي شاركها ربيع العمر."

And the night waxed deep, and the chosen and the beloved was dark with the night, and his spirit was as a cloud unspent. And he cried again:

"Heavy-laden is my soul with her own ripe fruit;

Heavy-laden is my soul with her fruit;

Who now will come and eat and be fulfilled?

My soul is overflowing with her wine.

Who now will pour and drink and be cooled of the desert heat?

"Would that I were a tree flowerless and fruitless,

For the pain of abundance is more bitter than barrenness,

ودَجّ الليل، ولفَّتِ المختارَ الحبيبَ عَتَمةُ الليل، وروحه غيمة لم تصُب. وطفَق ينوح من جديد:

"مثقلةٌ روحي بيانع ثمارها؛

مثقلةٌ بثمارها الروح؛

هل من يأتي الآنَ ويَطعَمُ ويرتوي؟

روحي تفيض بخمرتها.

هل من يصبّ ويتبرد من لظى الهجير؟

"ليتني كنت شجرة بلا ثمر ولا زهر،

فألم الوفر أشد مرارة من القفر،

129

And the sorrow of the rich from whom no one will take

Is greater than the grief of the beggar to whom none would give.

"Would that I were a well, dry and parched, and men throwing stones into me;

For this were better and easier to be borne than to be a source of living water

When men pass by and will not drink.

"Would that I were a reed trodden under foot,

For that were better than to be a lyre of silvery things

In a house whose lord has no fingers

And whose children are deaf."

وحزن الغني لا يجد من يأخذ منه

لأعظم من كَرَب الشحاذ لا يجد من يعطيه.

"ليتني كنت بئراً، ناضبة عطشى، يمطرني بالحجارة العابرون؛

لأفضل وأهون من أن أكون نبع ماء حي

يمر به الناس ولا يشربون.

"ليتني كنت قصبة تدوسها الأقدام،

لأحسن من قيثارة فضية النمنمات

في منزلٍ سيدُه بلا أصابع

وأبناؤه طرش."

Now, for seven days and seven nights no man came nigh the Garden, and he was alone with his memories and his pain; for even those who had heard his words with love and patience had turned away to the pursuit of other days.

Only Karima came, with silence upon her face like a veil; and with cup and plate within her hand, drink and meat for his aloneness and his hunger. And after setting these before him, she walked her way.

And Almustafa came again to the company of the white poplars within the gate, and he sat looking upon the road. And after a while he beheld as it were a cloud of dust blown above the road and coming toward him. And from out the cloud came the nine, and before them Karima guiding them.

ومرت أيام سبعة وليال سبع أمضى المختار الحبيب ساعاتها وحيداً مع ذكرياته وألمه، ولسبعة أيام وسبع ليال لم يقترب من الحديقة أحد؛ حتى الذين سمعوا كلماته بأناة وحب ولَّوا عنه ساعين لأيام أُخَر.

وحدها كريمة جاءت والصمت حجاب على وجهها؛ وبيدها وعاء وكوب، طعام وشراب لوحدته وجوعه. وبعدما وضعت ما حملته له أمامه، خرجت.

وعاد المصطفى إلى صحبة الحَور الأبيض في الحديقة، وجلس ينظر إلى الطريق. بعد هنيهة رأى كما بدا سحابة غبار تهب تجاهه. ومن قلب السحابة برز الرجال التسعة، تتقدمهم كريمة.

And Almustafa advanced and met them upon the road, and they passed through the gate, and all was well, as though they had gone their path but an hour ago.

They came in and supped with him at his frugal board, after that Karima had laid upon it the bread and the fish and poured the last of the wine into the cups. And as she poured, she besought the Master saying: 'Give me leave that I go into the city and fetch wine to replenish your cups, for this is spent.'

And he looked upon her, and in his eyes were a journey and a far country, and he said:

"Nay, for it is sufficient unto the hour."

خفَّ المصطفى ولاقاهم على الطريق، وعبَر البوابة بهم، وطاب لقاؤهم، فكأنهم لم يغادروه غير ساعة.

دخلوا واحتسَوا معه حول مائدته المقتصِدة، وجاءت كريمة بالسمك والخبز وصبت بقايا النبيذ. وفي الأثناء التمست المعلم قائلة:

"أستأذنك بالذهاب إلى السوق لأحضر شراباً للكؤوس، لقد نفِد هنا النبيذ."

رنا إليها، وفي عينيه رحلةٌ وبلّدٌ بعيد، وقال:

"لا عليكِ، يكفينا هذا زاداً الساعة."

And they ate and drank and were satisfied. And when it was finished, Almustafa spoke in a vast voice, deep as the sea and full as a great tide under the moon, and he said:

"My comrades and my road-fellows, we must needs part this day. Long have we sailed the perilous seas, and we have climbed the steepest mountains and we have wrestled with the storm. We have known hunger, but we have also sat at wedding-feasts. Oftentimes have we been naked, but we have also worn kingly raiment. We have indeed travelled far, but now we part. Together you shall go your way, and alone must I go mine.

"And though the seas and the vast lands shall separate us, still we shall be companions upon our journey to the Holy Mountain.

أكلوا وشربوا وارتَوَوا. بعدها تكلم المصطفى بصوت جهيرٍ، وكالبحرِ عميقٍ ومترعٍ كمدٍّ وجزرٍ تحت القمرِ عظيم، وقال:

"يا رفاقي وصحبةَ دربي، إني مفارقٌ اليوم. ركبت بحار المخاطر طويلاً. وتسلقت أعتى الجبال، وقارعت العاصفة. عرفت الجوع، وإن كنت جلست على موائد الأفراح. غالباً ما اعتريت، وإن كنت ارتديت ملابس تليق بأمير. قطعت أبعد المسافات، والآن أرحل. ستمضون في طريقكم معاً. وسأمضي في طريقي لوحدي.

"ورغم أن البحار والأمصار ستباعد بيننا، فلسوف نبقى في رحلتنا إلى الجبل المقدس رفاقاً.

"But before we go our severed roads, I would give unto you the harvest and the gleaning of my heart:

"Go you upon your way with singing, but let each song be brief, for only the songs that die young upon your lips shall live in human hearts.

"Tell a lovely truth in little words, but never an ugly truth in any words. Tell the maiden whose hair shines in the sun that she is the daughter of the morning. But if you shall behold the sightless, say not to him that he is one with night.

"Listen to the flute player as it were listening to April, but if you shall hear the critic and the fault-finder speak, be deaf as your own bones and as distant as your fancy.

"وقبل أن تفرقنا الدروب آحاداً، سأعطيكم حصاد قلبي وقشيشه:

"سيروا على دروبكم في غناء، واجعلوا الأغنية قصيرة، فالأغنيات التي تموت على الشفاه يافعة تحيا في قلب الإنسان.

"قولوا حقيقة حلوة بكلمات قليلة، ولا تقولوا حقيقة مرة بأية كلمات. قولوا للصَبية يضحك شعرها في الشمس إنها ابنة الصباح. وإن صادفتم الأعمى، لا تقولوا إنه صِنوُ الليل.

"أصغوا لعازف العود إصغاءَكم لنُوار، وإن سمعتم المنتقد ومتقصي الأخطاء، أعيروه أذناً صماء كما عظامكم الصماء وانأوا عنه نأيَ خيال.

139

"My comrades and my beloved, upon your way you shall meet men with hoofs; give them your wings. And men with horns; give them wreaths of laurel. And men with claws; give them petals for fingers. And men with forked tongues; give them honey for words.

"Ay, you shall meet all these and more; you shall meet the lame selling crutches; and the blind, mirrors. And you shall meet the rich men begging at the gate of the Temple.

"To the lame give your swiftness, to the blind of your vision; and see that you give of yourself to the rich beggars; they are the most needy of all, for surely no man would stretch a hand for alms unless he be poor indeed, though of great possessions.

"يا رفاقي وأحبتي، سيصادفكم رجال ذووا حوافر؛ أعطوهم أجنحتكم. ورجال ذووا قرون؛ أعطوهم أكاليلَ غار. ورجال ذووا مخالب؛ أعطوهم وروداً يجعلون منها أنامل. ورجال ألسنتهم مشعبة، أعطوهم عسلاً للكلام.

"أجل، ستصادفون كل هؤلاءٍ وأكثرَ من هؤلاء؛ ستصادفون الأعرجَ يبيع العُكاز؛ والأعمى يبيع المرآة. وعلى باب المعبد سترَون الأثرياء يتسولون الحسنات.

"أعط الأعرج خفتك، والأعمى من رؤاك؛ ولا تنس أن تعطي من ذاتك للمتسولين الأثرياء؛ هم أكثر حاجة من أي محتاج، فلا يمد رجل يده متسولاً إن لم يكن فقيراً بحق، رغم ما يحوزه من عظيم الممتلكات.

"My comrades and my friends, I charge you by our love that you be countless paths which cross one another in the desert, where the lions and the rabbits walk, and also the wolves and the sheep.

"And remember this of me: I teach you not giving, but receiving; not denial, but fulfilment; and not yielding, but understanding, with the smile upon the lips.

"I teach you not silence, but rather a song not over-loud.

"I teach you your larger self, which contains all men."

"يا رفاقي وأصدقائي، أناشدكم باسم محبتي لكم أن تكونوا دروباً لا تُعَد تتقاطع في البيداء حيث تجول الأسود والأرانب، وكذلك الأغنام والذئاب.

"وتذكروا هذا مني: لا أعلمكم العطاء، بل التلقي؛ لا أعلمكم الإنكار، بل الوفاء؛ لا أعلمكم الإذعان، بل الفهم، مع الابتسامة على الشفاه.

"لا أعلمكم الصمت، بل أغنيةً لا تبالغ في الصُّداح.

"أعلمكم ذاتَكم الأكبرَ، تلك التي تضمُ كلَ الرجال."

And he rose from the board and went out straightway into the Garden and walked under the shadow of the cypress-trees as the day waned. And they followed him, at a little distance, for their heart was heavy, and their tongue clave to the roof of their mouth.

Only Karima, after she had put by the fragments, came upon him and said:

"Master, I would that you suffer me to prepare food against the morrow and your journey."

And he looked upon her with eyes that saw other worlds than this, and said:

"My sister, and my beloved, it is done, even from the beginning of time. The food and the drink is ready, for the morrow, even as for our yesterday and our today.

ونهض عن المائدة وخرج إلى الحديقة ومشى تحت ظلال السرو والنهار إلى زوال. وتبعه الرجال، ولكن خطوات، فقلوبهم أُجهِدت، وألسنتهم التصقت بسقف الحلق.

وحدها كريمة دنت بعدما أزاحت الفتات، وقالت:

"أيها المعلم، أستأذنك بإعداد الطعام لغدك ورحلتك."

نظر إليها بعينين تريان إلى عوالم أخرى غير هذا العالم، وقال:

"أختاه، يا من جعلت لها في القلب مكاناً، الطعام والشراب جاهزان، حتى من بداية الزمان. جاهزان للغد، مثلما كانا للأمس واليوم.

"I go, but if I go with a truth not yet voiced, that truth will again seek me and gather me, though my elements be scattered throughout the silences of eternity, and again shall I come before you that I may speak with a voice born anew out of the heart of those boundless silences.

"And if there be aught of beauty that I have declared not unto you, then once again shall I be called, ay, even by mine own name, Almustafa, and I shall give you a sign, that you may know I have come back to speak all that is lacking, for God will not suffer Himself to be hidden from man, nor His word to lie covered in the abyss of the heart of man.

"I shall live beyond death, and I shall sing in your ears.

"إني ذاهب، فإن ذهبت بحقيقة لم أنطق بها، فثانية ستبحث عني تلك الحقيقة وتلتئمُ بي، رغم تناثر عناصري في الصمت اللانهائي، ولسوف آتي من جديد لأتكلم بصوت ولد للتو من قلب سكنات الخلود.

"فإن أغفلت قبَس جمال لم أفض به، فلسوف يناديني مناد، باسمي، المصطفى، أجل، ولسوف أومئ لكم لتعلموا أني عدت لأكمل ما قلت، فلن يرضى الله أن تُحجَب ذاتُه عن خلقه، ولا أن تتوارى كلمته في وَهدة القلب.

"سأحيا بعد الموت، وسأغني في آذانكم.

147

Even after the vast sea-wave carries me back

To the vast sea-depth.

I shall sit at your board though without a body,

And I shall go with you to your fields, a spirit
invisible.

I shall come to you at your fireside, a guest
unseen.

Death changes nothing but the masks that
cover our faces.

The woodsman shall be still a woodsman,

The ploughman, a ploughman,

And he who sang his song to the wind shall sing
it also to the moving spheres."

حتى بعد أن تحملني موجة البحر الكبرى وتعيدَني

إلى عمق-البحر الكبير.

سأجلس على موائدكم وإن بلا جسد،

وسأرافقكم إلى الحقول، روحاً لا تبصرها عين.

سآتيكم حول مواقدكم، ضيفاً لا تَرَون.

لا يغير الموت فينا شيئاً إلا الأقنعة التي تحجب الوجوه.

سيبقى الحطاب حطاباً،

والفلاح فلاحاً.

ومن صدح بأغنيته للريح سيغنيها أيضاً للفُلْك."

And the disciples were as still as stones, and grieved in their heart for that he had said: "I go." But no man put out his hand to stay the Master, nor did any follow after his footsteps.

And Almustafa went out from the Garden of his mother, and his feet were swift and they were soundless; and in a moment, like a blown leaf in a strong wind, he was far gone from them, and they saw, as it were, a pale light moving up to the heights.

And the nine walked their ways down the road. But the woman still stood in the gathering night, and she beheld how the light and the twilight were become one; and she comforted her desolation and her aloneness with his words: 'I go, but if I go with a truth not yet voiced, that very truth will seek me and gather me, and again shall I come.'

همَد الرجال همْدَ حجارة، وحزنت القلوب لسماع قوله 'إني ذاهب.' لكن أحداً لم يمد يده ملتمساً بقاءه، ولم يتقدم أحد وراءه.

وخرج المصطفى من حديقة أمه، بخطوٍ هينٍ وبلا صوت؛ وفي غمضة عين توارى، كما تتوارى ورقةٌ جرفتها ريح، ورأوا، كما بدا، نوراً وانياً يهُمُّ إلى المرتفعات.

وهبط التسعة الطريق. وحدها كريمة تأخرت، وقفت والليل يتكاثف حولها، وشاهدت التحام الشفق بالنور، بينما تواسي وحدتها وعزلتها بكلماته: 'إني ذاهب، فإن ذهبت بحقيقة لم أنطِق بها، فثانية ستبحث عني تلك الحقيقة وتلتئُم بي، وسآتيكم من جديد.'

AND now it was eventide.

And he had reached the hills. His steps had led him to the mist, and he stood among the rocks and the white cypress-trees hidden from all things, and he spoke and said:

"O Mist, my sister, white breath not yet held in a mould,

I return to you, a breath white and voiceless,

A word not yet uttered.

"O Mist, my winged sister mist, we are together now,

And together we shall be till life's second day,

Whose dawn shall lay you, dewdrops in a garden,

وأطبق المساء.

وكان قد بلغ التلال. وقاده خطوُه إلى الضباب، وبين الصخور وأشجار السرو الأبيض المحتجبة عن كل الأشياء، وقف، وتكلم وقال:

"يا غشاوة الضباب، يا شقيقتي، يا أنفاساً بيضاء لم يحدّها بعدُ إطار،

أعود إليك، نفَساً أبيضَ بلا صوت،

كلمةً لم ينطِق بها لسان.

"يا غشاوة الضباب، يا شقيقتي، يا ذات الجناح، نحن معاً الآن،

ومعاً سنبقى حتى اليوم الثاني في الحياة،

الذي فجرُه سينزّلك، قطراتِ ندىً في رياض،

153

And me, a babe upon the breast of a woman,

And we shall remember.

'O Mist, my sister, I come back, a heart listening in its depths.

Even as your heart,

A desire throbbing and aimless even as your desire,

A thought not yet gathered, even as your thought.

وينزلني طفلاً على صدر امرأة،

ولسوف نتذكر.

"يا غشاوة الضباب، يا شقيقتي، أعود قلباً يصغي في أعماقه،

مثلَ قلبك،

شوقاً يخفِق بلا غاية مثلَ شوقك،

هجساً بعد لم يلتئم، مثلَ هجسك.

"O Mist, my sister, first-born of my mother,

My hands still hold the green seeds you bade me scatter,

And my lips are sealed upon the song you bade me sing;

And I bring you no fruit, and I bring you no echoes

For my hands were blind, and my lips unyielding.

"O Mist, my sister, much did I love the world, and the world loved me,

For all my smiles were upon her lips, and all her tears were in my eyes.

"يا غشاوة الضباب، يا شقيقتي، وأولَ من ولدته أمي،

يداي لاتزالان قابضتين على البذور الخضرِ التي أوصيتِني بنثرها،

وشفتاي لاتزالان مطبِقتين على الأغنية التي أوصيتِني بأن أغني؛

لا أحمل لك ثماراً، ولا أصداء

يداي كانتا كفيفتين، وشفتاي عازفتين عن الكلام.

"يا غشاوة الضباب، يا شقيقتي، أحببت الدنيا كثيراً، وأحبتني الدنيا أيضاً،

كل ابتساماتي كانت على ثغرها، وكل دموعها في مقلتَيْ.

157

Yet there was between us a gulf of silence

which she would not abridge

And I could not overstep.

"O Mist my sister, my deathless sister Mist,

I sang the ancient songs unto my little children,

And they listened, and there was wondering
upon their face;

But tomorrow perchance they will forget the
song,

And I know not to whom the wind will carry
the song.

لكن هوة صمت انداحت بيننا أبت أن توجزَها

ولم أقدر أنا أن أتجاوزها.

"يا غشاوة الضباب، يا شقيقة لا تعرف الموت،

غنيت لأبنائي الصغار ألحان الأزل،

ولقد أصغَوا، والدهشة على وجوههم؛

ربما نسوا الأغنية غداً،

وأنا لا أعرف إلى من ستحمل الريحُ الأغنية.

And though it was not mine own, yet it came to my heart

And dwelt for a moment upon my lips.

"O Mist, my sister, though all this came to pass, I am at peace.

It was enough to sing to those already born.

And though the singing is indeed not mine,

Yet it is of my heart's deepest desire

ورغم أنها لم تكن أغنيتي، إلا أنها وصلت لقلبي،

وللحظة أقامت على شفتَي.

"يا غشاوة الضباب، يا شقيقتي، رغم أن ما مضى قد مضى، أجدني في سلام.

كفاني أني غنيت لمن ولدتهم الأرحام.

ورغم أن الغناء لم يكن غنائي،

إلا أنه من أعمق ما في قلبي من شوق.

"O Mist, my sister, my sister Mist,

I am one with you now.

No longer am I a self.

The walls have fallen,

And the chains have broken;

I rise to you a mist,

And together we shall float upon the sea until
life's second day.

When dawn shall lay you, dewdrops in a
garden,

And me a babe upon the breast of a woman."

"يا غشاوة الضباب، يا شقيقتي، يا شقيقة من ضباب،

أنا وأنتِ واحدٌ الآن.

لم أعد ذاتاً.

سقطت الجدران.

وتكسرت الأغلال؛

أصعد إليك ضباباً،

لنطوف فوق أديم البحر معاً حتى اليوم الثاني في الحياة.

حين ينزّلك الفجر، قطراتِ ندىً في رياض،

وينزلني طفلاً على صدر امرأة."

حديقة النبي

(هذا الكتاب يقرأ من اليسار)

تقديم

حديقة *النبي* هو الكتاب الثاني من ثلاثية بدأها جبران بكتاب *النبي* وكان ينوي أن يختمها بكتاب موت *النبي* لو لم يعاجله الموت قبل موت نبيه، ليخسر الإنسان في كل مكان فرصة نادرة أخرى لإغناء روحه والسمو بفكره والارتقاء بفهمه للوجود.

خلال ترجمتي لكتاب حديقة *النبي* الذي نشر بعد وفاة جبران بعام، لم ألحظ أي انعطاف عن الساقية الفكرية والروحية التي جرى عليها كتاب *النبي*. هناك عدد قليل جداً من إشارات التعجب التي خلا منها *النبي* تماماً، وأكاد أجزم بأن هذه الإشارات وضعت في حديقة *النبي* بقلم غير قلم جبران.

ما أريد أن أؤكده هنا هو أن حديقة *النبي* كتاب جبراني من ألفه إلى يائه. دفقة أصيلة من فكر جبران وروحه. السطر الأخير فيه لا يختلف في نبرته وزخمه وإيقاعه الكوني عن السطر الأول.

لم يشتغل على هذا الكتاب في قناعتي الراسخة أحد غير مؤلف *النبي*، باستثناء إشارات التعجب التي ذكرتها وأبقيت عليها في نص الترجمة

لملاحظة القارئ، والتزاماً مني بأمانة الترجمة التي يفرضها النص الذي أترجم منه، فأنا أراها إضافة وليس أصلاً.

هناك أمر آخر أود أن أقوله عن قناعة راسخة أيضاً وهو أني وجدت *حديقة النبي* محطة أقصى من *النبي* كمحطة على الطريق إلى الجبل القُدس الذي سار بنا عليها جبران في كل مؤلفاته الإبداعية، وفي هذا الكتاب- الثاني في الثلاثية التي لم تكتمل، اقترب بنا جبران إلى نقطة التماس بين الحياة والموت، حيث الحياة والموت واحد كما *النهر والبحر* *واحد*. *حديقة النبي* أكثر سبراً للغيب من *النبي*. *حديقة النبي* استمرار عالي البناء الدرامي والربط السردي لكتاب *النبي*.

صحيح أن *النبي*، الذي جابت أصداؤه الآفاق على مدى قرن ولاتزال، صعد بي إلى ذرى لم يحملني إليها أي كتاب غيره، لكن *حديقة النبي*، أوصلني إلى أفق أبعد، وكشف لي عن رؤية أوسع للطبيعة، ومنحني من ذات الطبيعة نشوة أعمق.

جميل العابد

نص جبران الإنكليزي يعثر على شكله العربي الأصلح

بقلم البروفسور بطرس الحلاق

أستاذ الأدب العربي المعاصر في جامعة السوربون

فيما كنت أقرأ ترجمة الأستاذ جميل، راح ينتابني شعور بأن الحلقة المفقودة بين وجهَي جبران، كاتباً بالعربية ثم كاتباً بالإنكليزية، بدأت تظهر للقارئ العربي، بعد فصام طويل جعل من مؤلف *النبي* شخصاً طارئاً في مسار جبران استأثر وحده بالعبقرية؛ مع ما في ذلك من إجحاف بحق وجهه الأول ومن تحجيم وتشويه لوجهه الثاني.

لم يترجم الأستاذ جميل بقدر ما اهتدى إلى ما كان يجول في فكر جبران وهو ينشئ عمله بلغة غير لغته، جاهداً في صياغة دفق قلبه المنساب بكل عفوية في لغته الأم، من خلال عبارات إنكليزية تقصر عن مدى الدفق الأصيل قصور الترجمة عن الإبداع بالسليقة، وكأني بالأستاذ جميل قد استبطن ذلك الدفق ليسكبه في لغة جبران التي تمثَّل حتى دقائقها بفضل ممارسته الطويلة لها. ولعلي أقول إنه شكّلها وصاغ صورتها التي يتمثل فيها المعنى وفق ما تراءى لجبران حينها. نعم، حينها. أي أنه لم يجمّد أسلوب جبران على الصيغة التي بدت في كتاباته العربية، بل شكلها وصاغ صورتها ليسكبها في قالب جبراني متطور

iii

اغتنى بخبرة سنين من الإبداع والتأمل وبقي مراعياً لخصوصيته الفذة: أسلوب جبران الأربعيني، هو، في آن معاً، نفسه وغيره بعد أن أنضجته الخبرة. لذا نجد فيه التيمات التي شغلت كتابته العربية.

وعلى سبيل المثال: ما قول الأستاذ جميل في ترجمته هنا عن شرط قيام الأمة *'أشفقوا على الأمة التي ترتدي ثوباً لا تنسجه، وتأكل خبزاً لا تحصده، وتشرب نبيذاً لا تعصر عنه'* إلا صدى لقول سابق مسنَد لجبران: "*ويل لأمة تأكل مما لا تزرع، وتشرب مما لا تعصر، وتلبس ما لا تنسج،*" وما قوله في شرط تكوُّن الفرد *' هكذا سيذوب ثلج قلبك حين ربيعك يأتي، وهكذا سيترقرق سرك سواقي تبحث في الوادي عن نهر الوجود، وسوف يحضن النهر سرك ويمضي به إلى البحر الكبير'،* إلا تذكيراً بمسار راوي *الأجنحة المتكسرة* الذي يتدرج من الجهل والإحساس المتهيج إلى المعرفة والعاطفة، وبالتالي إلى الحرية والحب؛ وعندها يتحول من "*حوض ماء منحبس بين الجبال إلى جدول يسير مترنماً إلى البحر.*"

أقر بأني وجدت في نص الأستاذ جميل، من حيث لا يدري، سنداً قوياً لمقولتي بأن عالم جبران هو ذاته منذ أول كلمة خطها بالعربية إلى آخر كلمة كتبها بالإنكليزية. عالم يصدر عن حدس فذّ استقاه من جغرافية شرقه ومن ثقافته التليدة التي غب منها عبر تراثه العربي، التراث الذي

تقصاه من أعماقه فقرأه قراءة دينامية بامتياز، أي في تشكله عبر مخاض طويل من زخم ثقافات ساميّة وشرقية توالت على هذه البقعة خلال آلاف السنين وأنتجت كبرى السرديات الإنسانية من نصوص دينية وملاحم بقيت فاعلة في ذاكرة اللغة الخفية وحية في الذاكرة الشعبية ومتخيلها. فإذا كانت كتابته العربية مستمدة من منابع التراث الثرة، فإن كتابته بالإنكليزية متولدة هي أيضاً من رحم كتابته العربية، إنما وفق سياق ثقافي آخر ومرحلة تاريخية محددة من عمر الإنسانية.

إن تراثنا العربي هو غير ما رآه فقهاء الأدب واللغة قديماً أو فقهاء الفكر الحداثي راهناً. ولا شك عندي أن جبران هو من أوائل الذين كشفوا عن الجوهر المكنوز في تراثنا العربي–العالمي الرائع. إنه وبكل تأكيد أكثر من مصلح اجتماعي عادي، وهو في آن غريب عن مفهوم النبوة الشائع الذي قد يخرجه من الشرط الإنساني. إنما هو إنسان من لحمنا ودمنا. حاول استقصاء معنى أن نكون في كل عصر، متجاوزاً معاً فخّ الشوفينية القومجية والعقائدية، ومفهوم "التقدم" المبني على العقلانية الصرفة التي تكاد تؤول إلى استعباد صرف. إنه الكاشف عن الدفق الحيوي في مصادرنا التراثية، الرحبة رحابة الشرق تاريخاً وجغرافيةً، وقد يكون المعبَر عن أحلامنا القصوى، ليس فقط بوصفنا عرباً–شرقاً، بل أيضاً بوصفنا شركاء في أحلام الإنسان المعاصر، أياً كانت ثقافتُه

وانتماؤه الديني والعقائدي، التائق إلى تجاوز القطيعة بين العقل والقلب، بين التقدم التقني والسمو الإنساني.

ألا نرى مع جبران أن الكينونة حركية لا تنقطع، وأن الحياة "تَشَكُّلٌ" مستمر على صورة الأفضل؟ يقول جبران في ترجمة الأستاذ جميل: "فنحن لسنا في الحقيقة بحكماء ولا بأغبياء. بل أوراق خضراء على شجرة الحياة، والحياة ذاتها أبعد من الحكمة، ولا شك أبعد من الغباء." ويقول في ذات الترجمة: "إن كنت تصبو إلى الحرية، فصِر إلى ضباب. عديمُ الشكل إلى الأبد يبحث عن شكل، كما السُدم التي لا تعَد، تصير إلى شموس وأقمار." ما أجمل ترجمتك، أستاذ جميل!

بطرس الحلاق
باريس في 21 تشرين الثاني 2019

vi

إلى غريتا ثنبِرغ

الفهرس

جميل العابد مترجم سوري-بريطاني عمل مخرجاً ومذيعاً في بي بي سي ثم معلماً للترجمة في جامعة ليدز. ترجم من الإنكليزية إلى العربية ونشر حتى الآن كتابين لجبران خليل جبران هما النبي وحديقة النبي. نال جائزة المفوضية الأوروبية للترجمة الإبداعية تلتها منحة إقامة للبحث الأدبي في جامعة إيست أنغليا. عضو المعهد البريطاني للترجمة والترجمة الفورية ITI.

حديقة النبي

جبران خليل جبران

إنكليزي - عربي

نقله

جميل العابد

Lightning Source UK Ltd.
Milton Keynes UK
UKHW010920150520
363293UK00002B/10/J

9 780992 899561